Immortal Songs of Camp and Field

CONTENTS

Bunker Hill Monument

Washington Monument

Flag of the brave!   Thy folds shall fly,
The sign of hope and triumph high!
When speaks the signal trumpet tone
And the long line comes gleaming on
(Ere yet the life-blood warm and wet
Has dimmed the glistening bayonet),
Each soldier eye shall brightly turn
To where thy sky-born glories burn,
And, as his springing steps advance,
Catch war and vengeance from the glance.
And when the cannon mouthing cloud
Heaves in wild wreaths the battle shroud,
And gory sabres rise and fall,
Like shoots of flame on midnight's pall;
There shall thy meteor-glances glow,
    And cowering foes shall shrink beneath
Each gallant arm that strikes below
    That lovely messenger of death.

Flag of the seas!   On ocean wave
Thy stars shall glitter o'er the brave;
When death, careering on the gale,
Sweeps darkly round the bellied sail,
And frighted waves rush wildly back
Before the broadside's reeling rack,
Each dying wanderer of the sea
Shall look at once to heaven and thee,
And smile to see thy splendors fly
In triumph o'er his closing eye.

18

Flag of the free heart's hope and home,
  By angel hands to valor given;
Thy stars have lit the welkin dome
  And all thy hues were born in heaven!
As fixed as yonder orb divine,
  That saw thy bannered blaze unfurled,
Shall thy proud stars resplendent shine,
  The guard and glory of the world.

—Joseph Rodman Drake.

The author of *The American Flag* was born to poverty, but by hard work he obtained a good education, and studied medicine under Dr. Nicholas Romayne, by whom he was greatly beloved. He obtained his degree and shortly afterward, in October, 1816, he was married to Sarah Eckford, who brought him a good deal of wealth. Two years later, his health failing, he visited New Orleans for the winter, hoping for its recovery. He returned to New York in the spring, only to die in the following autumn, September, 1820, at the age of twenty-five. He is buried at Hunt's Point, in Westchester County, New York, where he spent some of the years of his boyhood. On his monument are these lines, written by his friend, Fitz-Green Halleck,—

  "None knew him but to love him,
    Nor named him but to praise."

Drake was a poet from his childhood. The anecdotes preserved of his early youth show the fertility of his imagination. His first rhymes were a conundrum which he perpetrated when he was but five years old. He was one day, for some childish offense, punished by imprisonment in a portion of the garret shut off by some wooden bars. His sisters stole up to witness his suffering condition, and found him pacing the room, with something like a sword on his shoulder, watching an incongruous heap on the floor, in the character of Don Quixote at his vigils over the armor in the church. He called a boy of his acquaintance, named Oscar, "Little Fingal;" his ideas from books thus early seeking embodiment in living shapes. In the same spirit the child listened with great delight to the stories of an old neighbor lady about the Revolution. He would identify himself with the scene, and once, when he had given her a very energetic account of a ballad which he had read, upon her remarking that it was a tough story, he quickly replied, with a deep sigh: "Ah! we had it tough enough that day, ma'am."

Drake wrote *The Mocking-Bird*, one of his poems which has lived and will live, when a mere boy. It shows not only a happy facility but an unusual knowledge of the imitative faculty in the young poets of his time.

The American Flag was written in May, 1819, when the author was not quite twenty-four. It has

all his poems which could be found and took them to him. "See, Joe," said he to him, "what I have done." "Burn them," he replied; "they are value-less."

Drake's impulsive nature, as well as the spirit and force, yet simplicity, of expression, with his artless manner, gained him many friends. He had that native politeness which springs from benevo-lence — that would stop to pick up the hat or the crutch of an old servant, or fly to the relief of a child. His acquaintance with Fitz-Green Halleck arose in a romantic incident on the Battery one day when, in a retiring shower, the heavens were spanned by a rainbow. DeKay and Drake were together, and Halleck, a new acquaintance, was talking with them; the conversation taking the turn of some passing expression of the wishes of the moment, Halleck whimsically remarked that it would be heaven for him, just then, to ride on that rainbow and read Campbell. The idea was very pleasing to Drake. He seized Halleck by the hand and from that moment until his untimely death they were bosom friends.

The fame of our arms, of our laws the mild sway,
Had justly ennobled our nation in story,
Till the dark clouds of faction obscured our young
    day,
And enveloped the sun of American glory.
        But let traitors be told,
        Who their country have sold,
And bartered their God for his image in gold,
That ne'er will the sons of Columbia be slaves,
While the earth bears a plant, or the sea rolls its
    waves.

While France her huge limbs bathes recumbent in
    blood,
And society's base threats with wide dissolution;
May peace, like the dove who return'd from the flood,
Find an ark of abode in our mild constitution.
        But, though peace is our aim,
        Yet the boon we disclaim,
If bought by our sovereignty, justice, or fame;
For ne'er shall the sons of Columbia be slaves,
While the earth bears a plant, or the sea rolls its
    waves.

'Tis the fire of the flint each American warms:
Let Rome's haughty victors beware of collision;
Let them bring all the vassals of Europe in arms,
We're a world by ourselves, and disdain a provision.
        While with patriot pride
        To our laws we're allied,

No foe can subdue us, no faction divide;
For ne'er shall the sons of Columbia be slaves,
While the earth bears a plant, or the sea rolls its
    waves.

Our mountains are crown'd with imperial oak,
Whose roots, like our liberties, ages have nourish'd;
But long ere our nation submits to the yoke,
Not a tree shall be left on the field where it
    flourish'd.
        Should invasion impend,
        Every grove would descend
From the hilltops they shaded our shores to defend;
For ne'er shall the sons of Columbia be slaves,
While the earth bears a plant, or the sea rolls its
    waves.

Let our patriots destroy Anarch's pestilent worm,
Lest our liberty's growth should be check'd by cor-
    rosion;
Then let clouds thicken round us: we heed not the
    storm;
Our realm fears no shock, but the earth's own ex-
    plosion.
        Foes assail us in vain,
        Though their fleets bridge the main,
For our altars and laws with our lives we'll maintain;
For ne'er shall the sons of Columbia be slaves,
While the earth bears a plant, or the sea rolls its
    waves.

Should the tempest of war overshadow our land,
Its bolts could ne'er rend Freedom's temple asunder;
For, unmov'd, at its portal would Washington stand,
And repulse with his breast the assaults of the
    thunder!
        His sword from the sleep
        Of its scabbard would leap,
And conduct, with its point, every flash to the deep;
For ne'er shall the sons of Columbia be slaves,
While the earth bears a plant, or the sea rolls its
    waves.

Let Fame to the world sound America's voice;
No intrigues can her sons from their government
    sever:
Her pride is her Adams, their laws are his choice,
And shall flourish till Liberty slumbers forever.
        Then unite heart and hand,
        Like Leonidas' band,
And swear to the God of the ocean and land,
That ne'er shall the sons of Columbia be slaves,
While the earth bears a plant, or the sea rolls its
    waves.
               —Robert Treat Paine.

The father of the author of *Adams and Liberty*,
or as it has been more usually entitled in later
days, *Ye Sons of Columbia*, was the Robert Treat
Paine who was one of the immortal signers of
the Declaration of Independence. The author of

STATUE OF THE MINUTEMAN AT CONCORD, MASSACHUSETTS

this hymn was given by his parents the name of
Thomas, but on account of that being the name of
a notorious infidel of his time, he appealed to the
legislature of Massachusetts to give him a *Christian*
name; thereafter he took the name of his father,
Robert Treat Paine.

He was a very precocious and brilliant youth.
When he was seven years of age his family removed
from Taunton, where he was born, to Boston, and
there he prepared for Harvard College at one of the
public schools, entering the freshman class in his
fifteenth year. One of his classmates wrote a squib
on him in verse on the college wall, and Paine, on
consultation with his friends, being advised to re-
taliate in kind, did so, and thus became aware of the
poetic faculty of which he afterward made such
liberal use. He wrote nearly all his college com-
positions in verse, with such success that he was
assigned the post of poet at the College Exhibition
in the autumn of 1791, and at the Commencement
in the following year. After receiving his diploma,
he entered the counting-room of Mr. James Tisdale,
but soon proved that his tastes did not lie in that
direction. He would often be carried away by day-
dreams and make entries in his day-book in poetry.
On one occasion when he was sent to the bank with
a check for five hundred dollars, he met some liter-
ary acquaintances on the way and went off with
them to Cambridge, and spent a week in the enjoy-

ment of "the feast of reason and the flow of soul," returning to his duties with the cash at the end of that period.

In 1792 young Paine fell deeply in love with an actress, a Miss Baker, aged sixteen, who was one of the first players to appear in Boston. Their performances were at first called dramatic recitations to avoid a collision with a law forbidding "stage plays." He married Miss Baker in 1794, and was promptly turned out of doors by his father.

The next year, on taking his degree of A.M. at Cambridge, he delivered a poem entitled *The Invention of Letters*. There was a great deal of excitement over this poem at the time, as it contained some lines referring to Jacobinism, which the college authorities crossed out, but which he delivered as written. The poem was greatly admired, and Washington wrote him a letter in appreciation of its merits. It was immediately published and large editions sold, the author receiving fifteen hundred dollars as his share of the profits, which was no doubt a very grateful return to a poet with a young wife and an obdurate father. The breach with his family, however, was afterward healed.

Mr. Paine was also the author of a poem entitled *The Ruling Passion*, for which he received twelve hundred dollars. Still another famous poem of his was called *The Steeds of Apollo*.

In 1794 he produced his earliest ode, *Rise, Colum-*

bia, which, perhaps, was the seed thought from which later sprang the more extended hymn,—

" When first the sun o'er ocean glow'd
   And earth unveil'd her virgin breast,
Supreme 'mid Nature's vast abode
   Was heard th' Almighty's dread behest :
      ' Rise, Columbia, brave and free,
         Poise the globe, and bound the sea.' "

His most famous song, *Adams and Liberty*,— which is sung to the same tune as Key's *Star-Spangled Banner*, or *Anacreon in Heaven*,— was written four years later at the request of the Massachusetts Charitable Fire Society. Its sale yielded him a profit of more than seven hundred and fifty dollars. These receipts show an immediate popularity which has seldom been achieved by patriotic songs. In 1799 he delivered an oration on the first anniversary of the dissolution of the alliance with France which was a great oratorical triumph. The author sent a copy, after its publication, to Washington, and received a reply in which the General says: " You will be assured that I am never more gratified than when I see the effusions of genius from some of the rising generation, which promises to secure our national rank in the literary world; as I trust their firm, manly, and patriotic conduct will ever maintain it with dignity in the political."

35

The next to the last stanza of *Adams and Liberty* was not in the song as originally written. Paine was dining with Major Benjamin Russell, when he was reminded that his song had made no mention of Washington. The host said he could not fill his glass until the error had been corrected, whereupon the author, after a moment's thinking, scratched off the lines which pay such a graceful tribute to the First American: —

" Should the tempest of war overshadow our land,
　Its bolts could ne'er rend Freedom's temple
　　asunder;
　For, unmov'd, at its portal would Washington
　　stand,
　And repulse with his breast the assaults of the
　　thunder!
　　　His sword from the sleep
　　　Of its scabbard would leap,
　And conduct, with its point, every flash to the
　　deep;
　For ne'er shall the sons of Columbia be slaves,
　While the earth bears a plant, or the sea rolls its
　　waves.''

Instead of being added to the hymn it was inserted as it here appears. The second, fourth, and fifth stanzas have been usually omitted in recent publications of the hymn.

The brilliant genius of Paine was sadly eclipsed

And gave his orders to the men,—
  I guess there was a million.

And then the feathers in his hat,
  They were so tarnal fine-ah,
I wanted peskily to get
  To hand to my Jemima.

And then they'd fife away like fun
  And play on cornstalk fiddles;
And some had ribbons red as blood
  All wound about their middles.

The troopers, too, would gallop up,
  And fire right in our faces;
It scared me a'most to death
  To see them run such races.

And then I saw a snarl of men
  A-digging graves, they told me,
So tarnal long, so tarnal deep,—
  They allowed they were to hold me.

It scared me so I hooked it off,
  Nor stopped as I remember,
Nor turned about, till I got home,
  Locked up in mother's chamber.

It is certainly the tune of *Yankee Doodle*, and not the words of this old song, which captured the fancy of the country and held its sway in America for nearly a hundred and fifty years.

43

who was said to have ridden into Oxford on a small horse with his single plume fastened into a sort of knot which was derisively called a " macaroni." The words were,—

> " Yankee Doodle came to town,
>   Upon a Kentish pony;
> He stuck a feather in his cap,
>   Upon a macaroni."

Doctor Shuckburg at once began to plan a joke upon the uncouth newcomers. He set down the notes of *Yankee Doodle*, wrote along with them the lively travesty upon Cromwell, and gave them to the militia musicians as the latest martial music of England. The band quickly caught the simple and contagious air which would play itself, and in a few hours it was sounding through the camp amid the laughter of the British soldiers. It was a very prophetic piece of fun, however, which became significant a few years later. When the battles of Concord and Lexington began the Revolutionary War, the English, when proudly advancing, played along the road *God save the King;* but after they had been routed, and were making their disastrous retreat, the Americans followed them with the taunting *Yankee Doodle.*

It was only twenty-five years after Doctor Shuckburg's joke when Lord Cornwallis marched into the lines of these same old ragged Continentals to

FRANCIS SCOTT KEY

And where is that band who so vauntingly swore
That the havoc of war and the battle's confusion
A home and a country should leave us no more?
Their blood has washed out their foul footsteps'
 pollution.
　　　No refuge could save
　　　The hireling and slave
From the terror of flight or the gloom of the grave;
And the star-spangled banner in triumph doth wave
O'er the land of the free and the home of the brave!

Oh, thus be it ever when freemen shall stand
Between their loved homes and the war's desolation!
Blessed with victory and peace, may the heaven-
 rescued land
Praise the Power that hath made and preserved us
 a nation.
　　　Then conquer we must,
　　　When our cause it is just,
And this be our motto — " In God is our trust:"
And the star-spangled banner in triumph shall wave
O'er the land of the free and the home of the brave!

　　　　　　　　—Francis Scott Key.

No song could have had a more inspiring source
of creation than did this. Its author, Mr. Francis
Scott Key, was a young lawyer who left Baltimore
in September, 1814, while the war of 1812 was yet
going on, and under a flag of truce visited the

FORT McHENRY

during our civil war, there being no verse alluding
to treasonable attempts against the flag. It was
originally printed in the Boston *Evening Transcript*.

" When our land is illumined with liberty's smile,
   If a foe from within strike a blow at her glory,
   Down, down with the traitor who dares to defile
   The flag of her stars and the page of her story!
       By the millions unchained
       Who their birthright have gained
   We will keep her bright blazon forever unstained;
   And the star-spangled banner in triumph shall
     wave
   While the land of the free is the home of the
     brave.''

The air selected under such interesting circum-
stances as we have described — *Anacreon in
Heaven*, — is that of an old English song. In the
second half of the eighteenth century a jovial
society, called the '' Anacreontic,'' held its festive
and musical meetings at the '' Crown and Anchor ''
in the Strand. It is now the '' Whittington Club; ''
but in the last century it was frequented by Doctor
Johnson, Boswell, Sir Joshua Reynolds and others.
One Ralph Tomlinson, Esq., was at that time presi-
dent of the Anacreontic Society, and wrote the
words of the song adopted by the club, and John
Stafford Smith set them to music, it is claimed to
an old French air. The song was published by the

composer, and was sold at his house, 7 Warwick Street, Spring Garden, London, between the years 1770-75. Thus the source of the music so long identified with this inspiring song is swallowed up in the mystery of the name of Smith.

The flag of Fort McHenry, which inspired the song, still exists in a fair state of preservation. It is at this time thirty-two feet long and of twenty-nine feet hoist. In its original dimensions it was probably forty feet long; the shells of the enemy, and the work of curiosity hunters, have combined to decrease its length. Its great width is due to its having fifteen instead of thirteen stripes, each nearly two feet wide. It has, or rather had, fifteen five-pointed stars, each two feet from point to point, and arranged in five indented parallel lines, three stars in each horizontal line. The Union rests in the ninth, which is a red stripe, instead of the eighth, a white stripe, as in our present flag. There can be no doubt as to the authenticity of this flag. It was preserved by Colonel Armstead, and bears upon its stripes, in his autograph, his name and the date of the bombardment. It has always remained in his family and in 1861 his widow bequeathed it to their youngest daughter, Mrs. William Stuart Appleton, who, some time after the bombardment, was born in Fort McHenry under its folds. She was named Georgiana Armstead for her father, and the precious flag was hoisted on its staff in honor of her birth. Mrs. Appleton died in New York, July 25, 1878, and bequeathed the flag to her son, Mr. Eben Appleton, of Yonkers, New York, who now holds it.

The Star-Spangled Banner has come out of the Spanish War baptized with imperishable glory. Throughout the war it has been above all others, in camp or on the battlefield, the song that has aroused the highest enthusiasm. During the bombardment of Manila the band on a British cruiser, lying near the American fleet, played *The Star-Spangled Banner*, thus showing in an unmistakable way their sympathy with the American cause. In the trenches before Santiago it was sung again and again by our soldiers and helped, more than anything else, to inspire them to deeds of heroic valor. Once when the army moved forward in the charge, the man who played the E-flat horn in the band left his place and rushed forward with the soldiers in the attacking column. Of course the band's place is in the rear. But this man, unmindful of everything, broke away and went far up the hill with the charge, carrying his horn over his shoulder, slung with a strap. For a time he went along unobserved, until one of the officers happened to see him. And he said to him, "What are you doing here? You can't do anything; you can't fight; you haven't any gun or sword. This is no place for you. Get down behind that rock." The soldier fell back for a minute, half dazed, and feeling the pull of the strap on his shoulder cried out in agony: "I can't do anything, I can't fight." And so he got down behind the rock. But almost instantly he raised his horn and began to play *The Star-Spangled Banner*. They heard him down in the valley, and immediately the band took it up, and in the midst of those inspiring strains the army charged to victory.

JOSEPH HOPKINSON

HAIL COLUMBIA.

Hail, Columbia! happy land!
Hail, ye heroes! heaven-born band!
  Who fought and bled in Freedom's cause,
  Who fought and bled in Freedom's cause,
And when the storm of war was gone,
Enjoy'd the peace your valor won.
  Let independence be our boast,
  Ever mindful what it cost;
  Ever grateful for the prize,
  Let its altars reach the skies.

     Firm, united, let us be,
     Rallying round our Liberty;
     As a band of brothers join'd,
     Peace and safety we shall find.

Immortal patriots! rise once more:
Defend your rights, defend your shore:
  Let no rude foe, with impious hand,
  Let no rude foe, with impious hand,
Invade the shrine where sacred lies
Of toil and blood the well-earn'd prize.
  While offering peace sincere and just,
  In Heaven we place a manly trust,
  That truth and justice will prevail,
  And every scheme of bondage fail.

afterward appointed judge of the United States District Court, an office held by his grandfather under the British Crown before the Revolutionary War, and to which his father had been chosen on the organization of the United States Judiciary in 1789. He retained this office until his death in 1842.

Mr. Hopkinson was still a young man, only twenty-eight years of age, when he wrote the song which will make his name honored as long as American liberty is remembered. It was in the summer of 1798, when a war with France was thought to be inevitable. Congress was in session in Philadelphia, discussing the advisability of a declaration of war, and many acts of hostility had actually occurred. England and France were at war already, and the people of the United States were divided into factions for the one side or the other. One party argued that policy and duty required Americans to take part with republican France; the other section urged the wisdom of connecting ourselves with England, under the belief that she was the great conservator of modern civilization, and that her triumph meant the rule of good principles and safe government. Both belligerents had been careless of our rights, and seemed to be forcing us from the just and wise policy of Washington, which was to maintain a strict and impartial neutrality between them. The prospect of a rupture with France was exceedingly offensive to that portion of the people who hoped for her success, and the violence of party spirit ran to the highest extreme.

Just at this time a young singer who was very popular in Philadelphia was to be given a benefit at one of the theaters. This young man was a school friend of Joseph Hopkinson. They had kept up their acquaintance after their school-days had passed, and one Saturday afternoon he called on Hopkinson to talk over with him his benefit which was announced for the following Monday. He said he had every prospect of suffering a loss instead of receiving a benefit from the performance; but that if he could get a patriotic song adapted to the tune of the *President's March*, then the popular air, he would no doubt have a full house. The poor fellow was almost in despair about it, as the poets of the theatrical corps had been trying to accomplish it, and had come to the conclusion that no words could be composed to suit the music of that march. The young lawyer told his friend that he would try what he could do for him. He came the next afternoon, and the song, *Hail Columbia*, was ready for him. It was announced on Monday morning, and the theater was crowded to overflowing, and so continued, night after night, for the rest of the season. The excitement about it grew so great that the song was not only encored but had to be repeated many times each night, the audience joining in the chorus. It was also sung at night in the

THE CAPITOL

streets by large crowds of citizens, which often included members of Congress and other distinguished public officials. The enthusiasm spread to other cities and the song was caught up and reëchoed at all kinds of public gatherings throughout the United States.

The object of Mr. Hopkinson in writing the song, in addition to doing a kind deed for his friend and schoolmate, was to arouse an American spirit which should be independent of and above the interests, passions, and policy of both belligerents, and look and feel exclusively for our own honor and rights. For this reason no allusion was made to France or England, or to the war which was raging between them, or to our indignation as to their treatment of us. It was this prudence which gave the song its universal popularity. It found equal favor with both parties, for neither could disown the loyal sentiments it inculcated. It was so purely American, and nothing else, that the patriotic feelings of every American heart responded to it.

The *President's March*, for which the poem was specially written and to which it was easily adapted, was composed in honor of President Washington, who then resided at 190 High Street, Philadelphia. The composer of the popular air was Philip Roth, a teacher of music. Not a great deal is left on record about him, but it is declared that he was a very eccentric character, familiarly known

73

as " Old Roat." It is also said that he took snuff immoderately. A claim has been set up for Professor Phyla, of Philadelphia, but the evidence favors Roth.

During the centennial year an autograph copy of *Hail Columbia* was displayed in the museum at Independence Hall, Philadelphia. This copy was written from memory, February 22, 1828, and presented to George M. Kein, Esq., of Reading, in compliance with a request made by him. This interesting manuscript has marginal notes, one of which informs us that the lines: —

" Behold the chief who now commands,
Once more to serve his country stands,
  The rock on which the storm will beat;
  The rock on which the storm will beat.
But, arm'd in virtue firm and true,
His hopes are fix'd on Heaven and you.
  When hope was sinking in dismay,
  And glooms obscured Columbia's day,
  His steady mind, from changes free,
  Resolved on death or liberty,"

refer to John Adams, who was President of the United States at the time *Hail Columbia* was written. Mr. Hopkinson also presented General Washington with an autograph copy of his poem, and received from him a complimentary letter of thanks, which is now in possession of his descendants.

THOMAS À BECKET

The winecup, the winecup bring hither,
And fill you it true to the brim;
May the wreaths they have won never wither
Nor the star of their glory grow dim.
May the service united ne'er sever,
But they to their colors prove true,
The Army and Navy forever,
Three cheers for the red, white, and blue,
 Three cheers for the red, white, and blue,
 Three cheers for the red, white, and blue,
  The Army and Navy forever,
 Three cheers for the red, white, and blue.

     —Thomas à Becket.

This splendid song, as popular, perhaps, as any
of America's patriotic hymns, was written in 1843
by a young actor named Thomas à Becket. He
was engaged at that time at the Chestnut Street
Theater, in Philadelphia. He was waited upon by
a Mr. D. T. Shaw, an acquaintance, who was also
an actor, with the request that he would write him
a song for his benefit night. Mr. Shaw had been
trying to write one for himself, but had made a sad
failure of it. He produced some patriotic lines, and
asked Mr. À Becket's opinion on them; he found
them ungrammatical and so deficient in measure as
to be totally unfit to be set to music. They went to
the house of a mutual friend, and there À Becket
wrote the two first verses in pencil, and sitting

STATUE OF LIBERTY

down at a piano in the room of the friend's house, he composed the melody. On reaching home that evening he added the third verse, wrote the symphonies and arrangements, made a fair copy in ink, and gave it to Mr. Shaw, requesting him not to give or sell a copy to any one.

A few weeks afterward Mr. À Becket left for New Orleans, and a little while later was greatly astonished to see a published copy of his song entitled, "*Columbia, the Gem of the Ocean*, written, composed, and sung by David T. Shaw, and arranged by T. à Becket, Esq." On his return to Philadelphia he sought out Mr. Willig, the publisher, who told him he had purchased the song from Mr. Shaw. Mr. À Becket produced the original copy in pencil, and claimed the copyright, which Mr. Willig admitted, making some severe remarks upon Shaw's conduct in the affair. A week later it appeared under its proper title, "*Columbia, the Gem of the Ocean*, written and composed by T. à Becket, and sung by D. T. Shaw." The song has been often printed under the title *The Red, White, and Blue*, and is very familiarly known as "The Army and Navy Song," from being peculiarly adapted to reunions of the two wings of the military department of the government.

Mr. E. L. Davenport, an eminent actor, sung the song nightly in London for many weeks, where it became very popular. It was printed there under the title *Britannia, the Pride of the Ocean.* On this account some people have supposed the English version to be the original, and ours merely an adaptation of it. That part of its title, "The Gem of the Ocean," belongs to the Emerald Isle, rather than to Columbia, and seems more appropriate to designate an island power like Great Britain than a continental power like the United States. However, it is beginning to look as though we might have islands of our own in abundance.

While red, white, and blue have for a long time been the ranking order of the colors of British national ensigns, with us *blue* — the blue of the union, the firmament of our constellation of stars — claims the first place on our colors, red the second, and white the third; so that for us the song should read,—

"When borne by the blue, red, and white,"

instead of,—

"When borne by the red, white, and blue."

These lapses are explained by the fact that the author was an Englishman by birth, and it was very natural that he should make them. Though written by a native-born Englishman, the song was thoroughly American in its inception and origin. In the English version, already referred to, the first line is altered to read,—

"Britannia, the pride of the ocean."

In these days of kindly fellowship with England, Americans are perfectly willing to share their song of " red, white, and blue " with their cousins across the water.

GEORGE POPE MORRIS

THE FLAG OF OUR UNION.

A song for our banner, the watchword recall
  Which gave the Republic her station:
" United we stand — divided we fall ! "
  It made and preserves us a nation.
The union of lakes, the union of lands,
  The union of States none can sever!
The union of hearts, the union of hands,
  And the Flag of our Union forever and ever,
  The Flag of our Union forever!

What God in his infinite wisdom designed,
  And armed with republican thunder,
Not all the earth's despots and factions combined
  Have the power to conquer or sunder.
The union of lakes, the union of lands,
  The union of States none can sever!
The union of hearts, the union of hands,
  And the Flag of our Union forever and ever,
  The Flag of our Union forever!

Oh, keep that flag flying! The pride of the van!
  To all other nations display it!
The ladies for union are to a — man!
  And not to the man who'd betray it.
Then the union of lakes, the union of lands,
  The union of States none can sever!

The union of hearts, the union of hands,
  And the Flag of the Union forever!

  —George P. Morris.

The author of *The Flag of our Union* was one
of the most distinguished journalists of the early
half of the nineteenth century in America. He
was for many years the editor of the *Mirror*,
which was in its time the best literary magazine in
the country. Such men as William Cullen Bryant,
Fitz-Green Halleck, Nathaniel P. Willis, Theodore
S. Fay, and Epes Sargent found in its pages a
chance to express the poetry, romance, and philoso-
phy which flowed from their brilliant and graceful
pens.

Morris was the author of many songs and poems
that have become household words throughout the
land. Who does not recall,—

  " Woodman, spare that tree!
    Touch not a single bough!
  In youth it sheltered me,
    And I'll protect it now.
  'Twas my forefather's hand
    That placed it near his cot:
  There, woodman, let it stand,
    Thy ax shall harm it not! "

And these other lines from *My Mother's Bible*,
equally well known,—

88

WEST POINT MILITARY ACADEMY
(N. E. corner of cadets' barracks)

" I'm with you once again, my friends,
　　No more my footsteps roam;
Where it began my journey ends,
　　Amid the scenes of home.
No other clime has skies so blue,
　　Or streams so broad and clear,
And where are hearts so warm and true
　　As those that meet me here?

" Since last, with spirits wild and free,
　　I pressed my native strand,
I've wandered many miles at sea,
　　And many miles on land;
I've seen fair realms of the earth,
　　By rude commotion torn,
Which taught me how to prize the worth
　　Of that where I was born.

" In other countries when I heard
　　The language of my own,
How fondly each familiar word
　　Awoke an answering tone!
But when our woodland songs were sung
　　Upon a foreign mart,
The vows that faltered on the tongue
　　With rapture thrilled the heart.

" My native land! I turn to you
　　With blessing and with prayer,
Where man is brave, and woman true
　　And free as mountain air.

> Long may our flag in triumph wave,
>   Against the world combined,
> And friends a welcome — foes a grave,
>   Within our borders find.''

In this song we see the spirit in which was written *The Flag of our Union*. Ten years before the War of the Rebellion, when the mutterings of the coming storm were already in the air, this poet and traveler, who had found his country's flag such an inspiration when roving in foreign lands, poured out his heart in this hymn to the Flag. It was set to music by William Vincent Wallace, and was very popular in war times. It is worthy of popularity so long as the Flag of the Union shall wave.

JOHN BROWN

JOHN BROWN'S BODY.

John Brown's body lies mouldering in the grave!
John Brown's body lies mouldering in the grave!
John Brown's body lies mouldering in the grave!
   His soul is marching on.
    Glory, glory hallelujah!
    Glory, glory hallelujah!
    Glory, glory hallelujah!
   His soul is marching on.

The stars of heaven are looking kindly down!
The stars of heaven are looking kindly down!
The stars of heaven are looking kindly down!
   On the grave of old John Brown!

He's gone to be a soldier in the army of the Lord!
He's gone to be a soldier in the army of the Lord!
He's gone to be a soldier in the army of the Lord!
   His soul is marching on.

John Brown's knapsack is strapped upon his back!
John Brown's knapsack is strapped upon his back!
John Brown's knapsack is strapped upon his back!
   His soul is marching on.

      —Charles S. Hall.

No prophet is ever able to foretell what will catch
the popular ear. The original John Brown song,

97

written by Miss Edna Dean Proctor, is certainly far more coherent and intelligible than the lines which have formed the marching song for over a million men, and have held their own through a generation. It is well worth repeating here: —

"John Brown died on the scaffold for the slave;
  Dark was the hour when we dug his hallowed grave;
  Now God avenges the life he gladly gave,
          Freedom reigns to-day!
          Glory, glory hallelujah,
          Glory, glory hallelujah,
          Glory, glory hallelujah.
        Freedom reigns to-day!

"John Brown sowed and the harvesters are we;
  Honor to him who has made the bondsman free;
  Loved evermore shall our noble ruler be,
          Freedom reigns to-day!

"John Brown's body lies mouldering in the grave;
  Bright o'er the sod let the starry banner wave;
  Lo! for the million he periled all to save,
          Freedom reigns to-day!

"John Brown's soul through the world is marching on;
  Hail to the hour when oppression shall be gone;
  All men will sing in the better day's dawn,
          Freedom reigns to-day!

" John Brown dwells where the battle's strife is o'er;
  Hate cannot harm him, nor sorrow stir him more;
  Earth will remember the martyrdom he bore,
        Freedom reigns to-day!

" John Brown's body lies mouldering in the grave;
  John Brown lives in the triumph of the brave;
  John Brown's soul not a higher joy can crave,
        Freedom reigns to-day! "

The more popular, if not more worthy, song of
John Brown's Body seems to have been of Massa-
chusetts origin at the commencement of the Civil
War. It was first sung in 1861. When the Massa-
chusetts Volunteers, commanded by Colonel Fletcher
Webster, a son of the famous Daniel Webster, were
camped on one of the islands in Boston Harbor,
some of the soldiers amused themselves by adapting
the words,—

" John Brown's body lies a-mouldering in the grave,
        His soul is marching on.
        Glory, glory hallelujah,
        His soul is marching on,"

to a certain air. Mr. Charles Sprague Hall, who is
the author of the lines as finally sung, says that when
the soldiers first began to sing it the first verse was
the only one known. He wrote the other verses,
but did not know where the first one came from.

The way was opened for this song through a campaign song heard from the lips of the Douglas, and the Bell, and the Everett Campaign Clubs, who, in order to spite Governor John A. Andrew, the famous war governor of Massachusetts, sang the following lines as they were marching through the streets of Boston, with their torches in hand,—

> " Tell John Andrew,
> Tell John Andrew,
> Tell John Andrew
> John Brown's dead.
> > Salt won't save him,
> > John Brown's dead.''

These lines are supposed to have been an imitation of the doggerel,—

> " Tell Aunt Rhody,
> Tell Aunt Rhody,
> Tell Aunt Rhody
> The old goose is dead.
> > Salt won't save him,
> > The old goose is dead.''

Great stress having been laid by the opponents of Governor Andrew upon the fact that John Brown was dead, the authors of the song spoken of took good care to assert that, while

" John Brown's body lies a-mouldering in the grave,
His soul is marching on.''

HARPER'S FERRY

This was the answer of those that sympathized with John Brown, a song which they flung at those who seemed to take delight in the fact that he was dead.

Thane Miller, of Cincinnati, heard the melody, which is perhaps the most popular martial melody in America, in a colored Presbyterian church in Charleston, South Carolina, about 1859, and soon after introduced it at a convention of the Young Men's Christian Association in Albany, New York, with the words,—

> " Say, brothers will you meet us,
> Say, brothers will you meet us,
> Say, brothers will you meet us,
>   On Canaan's happy shore?
> By the grace of God we'll meet you,
> By the grace of God we'll meet you,
> By the grace of God we'll meet you,
>   Where parting is no more."

Professor James E. Greenleaf, organist of the Harvard Church in Charlestown, found the music in the archives of that church, and fitted it to the first stanza of the present song. It has since been claimed that the Millerites, in 1843, used the same tune to a hymn, one verse of which is as follows,—

> " We'll see the angels coming
>   Through the old churchyards,
> Shouting through the air
>   Glory, glory hallelujah!"

Whatever may have been the origin of the melody, when fitted by Greenleaf to the first stanza of *John Brown's Body*, it became so great a favorite with the Glee Club of the Boston Light Infantry that they asked Mr. Hall to write the additional stanzas.

As has been the case with popular tunes in every age, verses have been often added to it to meet the occasion. While the words are not of a classical order, the air is of that popular kind which strikes the heart of the average man. During the Civil War it served to cheer and inspire the Union soldiers in their camps and on the march, and was sung at home at every popular gathering in town or country. It seemed to be just what the soldiers needed at the time, and served its purpose far better than would choicer words or more artistic music. No song during all the war fired the popular heart as did *John Brown's Body*. It crossed the sea and became the popular street song in London. The *Pall Mall Gazette* of October 14, 1865, said: "The street boys of London have decided in favor of *John Brown's Body*, against *My Maryland*, and *The Bonnie Blue Flag*. The somewhat lugubrious refrain has excited their admiration to a wonderful degree, and threatens to extinguish that hard-worked, exquisite effort of modern minstrelsy, *Slap Bang*."

After the original song had gained world-wide notoriety, the following words were written by

Henry Howard Brownell, who died at Hartford,
Connecticut, October 31, 1872, aged fifty-two. Mr.
Brownell entitled his poem, "Words that can be
sung to the *Hallelujah Chorus*," and says: "If
people will sing about Old John Brown, there is no
reason why they shouldn't have words with a little
meaning and rhythm in them."

"Old John Brown lies a-mouldering in the grave,
Old John Brown lies slumbering in his grave —
But John Brown's soul is marching with the brave,
    His soul is marching on.
        Glory, glory hallelujah!
        Glory, glory hallelujah!
        Glory, glory hallelujah!
    His soul is marching on.

"He has gone to be a soldier in the Army of the
    Lord,
He is sworn as a private in the ranks of the Lord —
He shall stand at Armageddon, with his brave
    old sword,
        When Heaven is marching on.

"He shall file in front where the lines of battle
    form —
He shall face the front where the squares of battle
    form —
Time with the column and charge with the storm,
        Where men are marching on.

"Ah, foul tyrants! do you hear him where he
    comes?
Ah, black traitors! do you know him as he comes?
In thunder of the cannon and roll of the drums,
        As we go marching on.

"Men may die, and moulder in the dust —
Men may die, and arise again from dust,
Shoulder to shoulder, in the ranks of the just,
        When Heaven is marching on."

But Mr. Brownell has shared the same fate with
Miss Proctor, and his song and hers are only curi-
osities to-day, which show how arbitrary the popu-
lar will is when once the heart or the imagination is
really captured. Mr. Richard Henry Dana, Jr.,
writing to Mr. James T. Fields, the famous Boston
litterateur, said: "It would have been past belief
had we been told that the almost undistinguishable
name of John Brown should be whispered among
four millions of slaves, and sung wherever the Eng-
lish language is spoken, and incorporated into an
anthem to whose solemn cadences men should
march to battle by the tens of thousands."

DIXIE.

date ? '59

I wish I was in de land ob cotton,
Old times dar am not forgotten,
 Look away! Look away! Look **away**!
In Dixie Land where I was born in,
Early on a frosty mornin,
 Look away! Look away! Look away!
  Den I wish I was in Dixie,
   Hooray! Hooray!
  In Dixie Land, I'll take my stand,
  To lib and die in Dixie,
   Away! Away!
  Away down south in Dixie.

Old Missus marry " Will-de-weaber,"
Willium was a gay deceaber;
 Look away! Look away! Look away.
But when he put his arm around 'er,
He smiled as fierce as a forty pounder,
 Look away! Look away! Look away!

His face was as sharp as a butcher's cleaber,
But dat did not seem to greab 'er;
 Look away! Look away! Look away!
Old Missus acted de foolish part,
And died for a man dat broke her heart.
 Look away! Look away! Look away!

Now here's a health to de next old Missus,
And all de gals dat want to kiss us;
    Look away! Look away! Look away!
But if you want to drive 'way sorrow,
Come and hear dis song tomorrow,
    Look away! Look away! Look away!

Dar's buckwheat cakes an' Injen batter,
Makes you fat or a little fatter;
    Look away! Look away! Look away!
Den hoe it down and scratch your grabble,
To Dixie's Land I'm bound to trabble,
    Look away! Look away! Look away!
            —Dan Emmett.

Dan Emmett, who wrote the original *Dixie*, which
has been paraphrased and changed and adapted
nearly as frequently as *Yankee Doodle* was born at
Mount Vernon, Ohio, in 1815. He came from a
family all of whose members had a local reputa-
tion, still traditional in that part of the country, as
musicians. In his own case this talent, if given a
fair chance for development, would have amounted
to genius. He began life as a printer, but soon
abandoned his trade to join the band of musicians
connected with a circus company. He was not
long in discovering that he could compose songs of
the kind in use by clowns; one of the most popular
of these was *Old Dan Tucker*. Its success was so

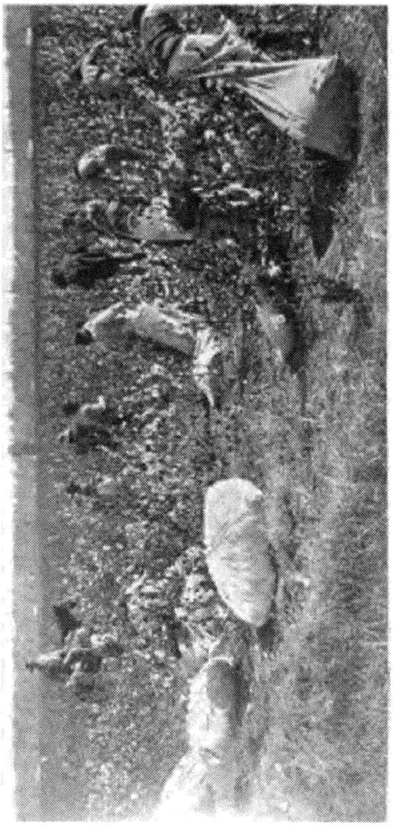

great that Emmett followed it with many others. They were all negro melodies, and many of them won great popularity. Finally he took to negro impersonations, singing his own songs in the ring, while he accompanied himself on the banjo. He made a specialty of old men, and he declares with pride that when he had blackened his face, and donned his wig of kinky white hair, he was "the best old negro that ever lived." He became such a favorite with the patrons of the circus in the South and West, that at last — partly by chance, and partly through intention — he became a full-fledged actor. This was in 1842, at the old Chatham Theater in New York City, when with two companions he gave a mixed performance, made up largely of songs and dances typical of slave life and character. The little troupe was billed as "The Virginia Minstrels," and their popularity with the public was instantaneous.

This was the beginning of negro minstrelsy, which was destined to have such a wide popularity in America. From New York the pioneer company went to Boston, and later on sailed for England, leaving the newly-discovered field to the host of imitators who were rapidly dividing their success with them. Emmett had great success in the British Isles, and remained abroad for several years. When he returned to New York, he joined the Dan Bryant Minstrel Company, which then held sway in Bryant's Theater on lower Broadway, which was at that time one of the most popular resorts in New York City. Emmett was engaged to write songs and walk-arounds and take part in the nightly performances. It was while he was with Bryant that *Dixie* was composed.

Emmett is still living and resides at Mount Vernon, Ohio, where he hopes to end his days. The old man is a picturesque figure on the streets. In his prime he was one of the mid-century dandies of New York City, but now, with calm indifference to the conventional, he usually carries a long staff and wears his coat fastened in at the waist by a bit of rope. His home is a little cottage on the edge of town, where he lives entirely alone. On almost any warm afternoon he can be found seated before his door reading, but he is ready enough to talk with the chance visitor whose curiosity to meet the composer of one of the National Songs of America, has brought him thither. A newspaper man who recently went to talk with the old minstrel found him seated in the shade by his house with a book open before him. As he went up the path, he said, for he had some doubt in his own mind, —

" Are you Dan Emmett, who wrote *Dixie?*"

" Well, I have heard of the fellow; sit down," and Emmett motioned to the steps.

" Won't you tell me how the song was written?"

" Like most everything else I ever did," said

Emmett, " it was written because it had to be done.
One Saturday night, in 1859, as I was leaving Bry-
ant's Theater, where I was playing, Bryant called
after me, ' I want a walk-'round for Monday, Dan.'

" The next day it rained and I stayed indoors.
At first when I went at the song I couldn't get any-
thing.   But a line,

' I wish I was in Dixie,'

kept repeating itself in my mind, and I finally took
it for my start.   The rest wasn't long in coming.
And that's the story of how *Dixie* was written.

" It made a hit at once, and before the end of the
week everybody in New York was whistling it.
Then the South took it up and claimed it for its
own.   I sold the copyright for five hundred dollars,
which was all I ever made from it.   I'll show you
my first copy."

He went into the house and returned in a moment
with a yellow, worn-looking manuscript in his hand.

" That's *Dixie*," he said, holding it up for in-
spection.   " I am going to give it to some historical
society in the South, one of these days, for though
I was born here in Ohio, I count myself a South-
erner, as my father was a Virginian."

Dixie Land was without question the most famous
of all the Southern war songs.   But it was the tune,
as in the case of *Yankee Doodle*, and not the words
that gave it its great power to fire the heart.   It is

claimed that Emmett appropriated the tune from an old negro air, which is quite probable.

The only poem set to the famous air of *Dixie* which has any literary merit is one that was written by General Albert Pike. Some one has said that it is worthy of notice that the finest Puritan lyric we have was written by an Englishwoman, Mrs. Felicia Hemans, and the most popular Southern war song was written by a Yankee, a native of Massachusetts. Albert Pike was born in Boston, December 29, 1809, but most of his boyhood was spent in Newburyport. He became a teacher, but in 1831 visited what was then the wild region of the Southwest with a party of trappers. He afterward edited a paper at Little Rock, and studied law. He served in the Mexican War with distinction, and on the breaking out of the Rebellion enlisted, on the Confederate side, a force of Cherokee Indians, whom he led at the battle of Pea Ridge. After the war he edited the Memphis *Appeal* till 1868, when he settled in Washington as a lawyer. He has written a number of fine poems, and retired from the profession of law in 1880, to devote himself to literature and Freemasonry. Mr. Pike's version of *Dixie* is as follows,—

" Southrons, hear your Country call you!
Up, lest worse than death befall you!
To arms! To arms! To arms, in Dixie!

116

ALBERT PIKE

Lo! all the beacon fires are lighted —
Let all hearts be now united!
    To arms! To arms! To arms, in Dixie!
        Advance the flag of Dixie!
           Hurrah! Hurrah!
        For Dixie's land we take our stand,
        And live or die for Dixie!
           To arms!   To arms!
        And conquer peace for Dixie!
           To arms!   To arms!
        And conquer peace for Dixie!

" Hear the Northern thunders mutter!
Northern flags in South winds flutter!
        To arms!
Send them back your fierce defiance!
Stamp upon the accursed alliance!
        To arms!
        Advance the flag of Dixie!

" Fear no danger! Shun no labor!
Lift up rifle, pike, and sabre!
        To arms!
Shoulder pressing close to shoulder,
 Let the odds make each heart bolder!
        To arms!
        Advance the flag of Dixie!

" How the South's great heart rejoices,
At your cannons' ringing voices!
        To arms!

For faith betrayed, and pledges broken,
Wrongs inflicted, insults spoken,
  To arms!
  Advance the flag of Dixie!

"Strong as lions, swift as eagles,
 Back to their kennels hunt these beagles!
  To arms!
Cut the unequal bonds asunder!
Let them hence each other plunder!
  To arms!
  Advance the flag of Dixie!

"Swear upon your country's altar
 Never to submit or falter!
  To arms!
Till the spoilers are defeated,
Till the Lord's work is completed.
  To arms!
  Advance the flag of Dixie!

"Halt not till our Federation
 Secures from earth's powers its station!
  To arms!
Then at peace, and crowned with glory,
Hear your children tell the story!
  To arms!
  Advance the flag of Dixie!

"If the loved ones weep in sadness,
 Victory soon will bring them gladness.
  To arms!

Exultant pride soon vanish sorrow;
Smiles chase tears away tomorrow.
> To arms! To arms! To arms, in Dixie!
> Advance the flag of Dixie!
> Hurrah! Hurrah!
> For Dixie's land we take our stand,
> And live or die for Dixie!
> To arms! To arms!
> And conquer peace for Dixie!
> To arms! To arms!
> And conquer peace for Dixie!"

Since the war *Dixie* has been as favorite a tune with bands of music throughout the North as has *Yankee Doodle*. Abraham Lincoln set the example for this. A war correspondent recalls an incident which occurred only a night or two before Mr. Lincoln was assassinated. The President had returned from Richmond, and a crowd called with a band to tender congratulations and a serenade. The great man who was so soon to be the victim of the assassin's bullet appeared in response to calls and thanked his audience for the compliment. Several members of his Cabinet surrounded him, and it was a very interesting and dramatic occasion. Just as he was closing his brief remarks, Mr. Lincoln said: " I see you have a band with you. I should like to hear it play *Dixie*. I have consulted the Attorney-General, who is here by my side, and he is of the opinion that Dixie belongs to us. Now play it."

The band struck up the old tune, and played it heartily. As the strains of the music rang out upon the air, cheer after cheer went up from the throats of the hundreds of happy men who had called to congratulate Mr. Lincoln upon the return of peace. It was that great soul's olive branch which he held out to the South.

ABRAHAM LINCOLN

THE BATTLE CRY OF FREEDOM.

Yes, we'll rally round the flag, boys, we'll rally once
again,
    Shouting the battle cry of Freedom,
We'll rally from the hillside, we'll gather from the
plain,
    Shouting the battle cry of Freedom!
    The Union forever, hurrah! boys, hurrah!
    Down with the traitor, up with the star,
    While we rally round the flag, boys, rally once
again,
    Shouting the battle cry of Freedom!

We are springing to the call of our brothers gone
before,
    Shouting the battle cry of Freedom;
And we'll fill the vacant ranks with a million free-
men more,
    Shouting the battle cry of Freedom!

We will welcome to our numbers the loyal, true, and
brave,
    Shouting the battle cry of Freedom;
And although they may be poor, not a man shall be
a slave,
    Shouting the battle cry of Freedom!

So we're springing to the call from the East and
    from the West,
        Shouting the battle cry of Freedom;
And we'll hurl the rebel crew from the land we love
    the best,
        Shouting the battle cry of Freedom!

                      —George F. Root.

This inspiring rallying song was written by George
F. Root, to whom we are indebted for so many
songs of camp and field. Mr. Root also composed
the music. Perhaps no hymn of battle in America
has been sung under so many interesting circum-
stances as this. It was written in 1861, on Presi-
dent Lincoln's second call for troops, and was first
sung at a popular meeting in Chicago and next at a
great mass meeting in Union Square, New York,
where those famous singers, the Hutchinson
Family, sounded it forth like a trump of jubilee to
the ears of thousands of loyal listeners.

It was always a great favorite with the soldiers.
Dr. Jesse Bowman Young, of St. Louis, the author
of *What a Boy Saw in the Army*, relates a very
affecting and pathetic incident which occurred while
a portion of the Army of the Potomac was marching
across Maryland. A young officer and his company
were in the lead, and just behind them came one
of the regimental bands, while ahead of them rode
General Humphreys and his staff. As the division

marched along, they passed by a country school-
house in a little grove at a crossroad. The teacher,
hearing the music of the band at a distance, and ex-
pecting the arrival of the troops, had dismissed the
school to give them a sight of the soldiers. Before
the troops came in sight the boys and girls had
gathered bunches of wild flowers, platted garlands
of leaves, and secured several tiny flags, and as
General Humphreys rode up in front of the school-
house, a little girl came forth and presented him
with a bouquet, which he acknowledged with gra-
cious courtesy. Then the group of assembled pupils
began to sing, as they waved their flags and gar-
lands in the air. That song made a tumult in every
soldier's heart. Many strong men wept as they
looked on the scene and thought of their own loved
ones far away in their Northern homes, and were
inspired with newborn courage and patriotism by
the sight and the song. This is the chorus which
rang forth that day from the country schoolhouse,
and which soon afterward echoed through the battle
in many a soldier's ear and heart, miles away, on
the bloody field of Gettysburg:—

" The Union forever, hurrah! boys, hurrah!
  Down with the traitor, up with the star,
  While we rally round the flag, boys, rally once
    again,
  Shouting the battle cry of Freedom! ' '

The first company that passed responded to their captain with a will as he shouted, " Boys, give them three cheers and a tiger!" and the example was imitated by the regiments that followed; so that amid the singing of the children and the cheers of the soldiers, and the beating of the drums, the occasion was made memorable to all concerned.

Richard Wentworth Browne relates that a day or two after Lee's surrender in April, 1865, he visited Richmond, in company with some other Union officers. After a day of sight-seeing, the party adjourned to Mr. Browne's rooms for dinner. After dinner one of the officers who played well opened the piano, saying, " Boys, we have our old quartette here, let's have a song." As the house opposite was occupied by paroled Confederate officers, no patriotic songs were sung. Soon the lady of the house handed Mr. Browne this note: " Compliments of General —— and staff. Will the gentlemen kindly allow us to come over and hear them sing?" Consent was readily given and they came. As the General entered the room, the Union officers recognized instantly the face and figure of an officer who had stood very high in the Confederacy. After introductions, and the usual interchange of civilities, the quartette sang for them glees and college songs, until at last the General said, " Excuse me, gentlemen, you sing delightfully, but what we want to hear is your army songs." Then they gave them the

FORT SUMTER

army songs with unction: *The Battle Hymn of the Republic; John Brown's Body; We're coming, Father Abraham; Tramp, Tramp, Tramp, the Boys are Marching;* and so on through the whole catalogue to the *Star-Spangled Banner*,—to which the Confederate feet beat time as if they had never stepped to any but the music of the Union,—and closed their concert with Root's inspiring *Battle Cry of Freedom.*

When the applause had subsided, a tall, fine-looking young fellow in a major's uniform exclaimed, "Gentlemen, if we'd had your songs we'd have licked you out of your boots! Who couldn't have marched or fought with such songs? while we had nothing, absolutely nothing, except a bastard Marseillaise, *The Bonny Blue Flag*, and *Dixie*, which were nothing but jigs.. *Maryland, my Maryland* was a splendid song, but the tune, old *Lauriger Horatius*, was about as inspiring as the Dead March in *Saul*, while every one of these Yankee songs is full of marching and fighting spirit."

Then turning to the General he said, "I shall never forget the first time I heard that chorus, 'Rally round the Flag.' It was a nasty night during the Seven Days' fight, and if I remember rightly, it was raining. I was on picket, when just before 'taps' some fellow on the other side struck up *The Battle Cry of Freedom* and others joined in the chorus until it seemed to me that the whole

saved for such a time as this, and now, by order of Abraham Lincoln, it was brought back to wave again over Fort Sumter. It was attached to the halyards, and General Anderson hoisted it to the head of the flagstaff amid loud huzzas. One can imagine the inspiration of the occasion, as William B. Bradbury led the singing of *The Battle Cry of Freedom*. How the tears ran down the cheeks, and hearts overflowed with thanksgiving as they shouted the chorus underneath the folds of the very flag that had received the first baptism of fire at the beginning of the Rebellion:—

" The Union forever, hurrah! boys, hurrah!
  Down with the traitor, up with the star,
    While we rally round the flag, boys, rally once
      again,
    Shouting the battle cry of Freedom!"

HENRY CLAY WORK

SONG OF A THOUSAND YEARS.

Lift up your eyes, desponding freemen!
  Fling to the winds your needless fears!
He who unfurl'd your beauteous banner,
  Says it shall wave a thousand years!
    " A thousand years!" my own Columbia,
      'Tis the glad day so long foretold!
     'Tis the glad morn whose early twilight,
      Washington saw in times of old.

What if the clouds, one little moment,
  Hide the blue sky where morn appears —
When the bright sun, that tints them crimson,
  Rises to shine a thousand years?

Tell the great world these blessed tidings!
  Yes, and be sure the bondman hears;
Tell the oppressed of every nation,
  Jubilee lasts a thousand years!

Envious foes, beyond the ocean!
  Little we heed your threat'ning sneers;
Little will they — our children's children —
  When you are gone a thousand years.

Rebels at home! go hide your faces —
  Weep for your crimes with bitter tears;

137

You could not bind the blessed daylight,
  Though you should strive a thousand years.

Back to your dens, ye secret traitors!
  Down to your own degraded spheres!
Ere the first blaze of dazzling sunshine,
  Shortens your lives a thousand years.

Haste thee along, thou glorious noonday!
  Oh, for the eyes of ancient seers!
Oh, for the faith of him who reckons
  Each of his days a thousand years!

                    —*Henry Clay Work.*

Henry Clay Work was born in Middletown, Connecticut, October 1, 1832. The family came originally from Scotland, and the name is thought to have come from a castle, "Auld Wark, upon the Tweed," famed in the border wars in the times made immortal by Sir Walter Scott. He inherited his love of liberty and hatred of slavery from his father, who suffered much for conscience' sake. While quite young, his family moved to Illinois, near Quincy, and he passed his boyhood in the most abject poverty, his father having been taken from home and imprisoned because of his strong anti-slavery views and active work in the struggles of those enthusiastic and devoted reformers. In 1845, Henry's father was pardoned on condition that he would leave the State of Illinois. The family then

returned to Connecticut. After a few months' at-
tendance at school in Middletown, our future song
writer was apprenticed to Elisha Geer, of Hartford,
to learn the printer's trade. He learned to write
over the printer's case in much the same way as did
Benjamin Franklin. He never had any music les-
sons except a short term of instruction in a church
singing school. The poetic temperament, and his
musical gifts as well, were his inheritance. He be-
gan writing very early, and many of his unambitious
little poems found their way into the newspapers
during his apprenticeship.

Work's first song was written in Hartford and
entitled, *We're coming, Sister Mary*. He sold this
song to George Christie, of Christie's minstrels, and
it made a decided hit. In 1855 he removed to Chi-
cago, where he continued his trade as a printer.
The following year he married Miss Sarah Parker,
of Hubbardston, Massachusetts, and settled at Hyde
Park. In 1860 he wrote *Lost on the " Lady Elgin,"*
a song commemorating the terrible disaster to a Lake
Michigan steamer, which became widely known.

Kingdom Coming was Work's first war song, and
was written in 1861. Now that it has been so suc-
cessful, it seems strange that he should have had
trouble to find a publisher for it; yet such was the
case. But its success was immediate as soon as
published. It is perhaps the most popular of all the
darkey songs which deal directly with the question

of the freedom of the slaves. It set the whole world
laughing, but there was about it a vein of political
wisdom as well as of poetic justice that commended
it to strong men. The music is full of life and
is as popular as the words. It became the song of
the newsboys of the home towns and cities as well
as of the soldiers in the camp and on the march. It
portrays the practical situation on the Southern
plantation as perhaps no other poem brought out
by the war:—

"Say, darkies, hab you seen de massa,
  Wid de muffstash on his face,
Go long de road some time dis mornin',
  Like he gwine to leab de place?
He seen a smoke way up de ribber,
  Whar de Linkum gunboats lay;
He took his hat, an' lef' bery sudden,
  An' I spec he's run away!
    De massa run? ha, ha!
    De darkey stay? ho, ho!
    It mus' be now de kingdom comin',
    And de year ob jubilo!

"He's six feet one way, two foot tudder,
  An' he weigh tree hundred poun',
His coat's so big he couldn't pay de tailor,
  An' it won't go half way roun'.
He drill so much dey call him cap'an,
  An' he get so drefful tann'd,

THE WHITE HOUSE

I spec he try an' fool dem Yankees
    For to t'ink he's contraband.

"De darkies feel so lonesome
    Libing in de log house on de lawn,
Dey moved dar tings to massa's parlor,
    For to keep it while he gone.
Dar's wine and cider in de kitchen,
    An' de darkies dey'll hab some;
I spose dey'll all be cornfiscated,
    When de Linkum sojers come.

"De oberseer he make us trubbel,
    An' he dribe us round a spell;
We lock him up in de smoke-house cellar,
    Wid de key trown in de well.
De whip is lost, de handcuff's broken,
    But de massa'll hab his pay;
He's ole enough, big enough, ought to known
      better,
    Den to went an' run away."

Another most popular slave song which had a tremendous sale was entitled *Wake Nicodemus*, the first verse of which is,—

" Nicodemus, the slave, was of African birth,
    And was bought for a bagful of gold;
He was reckon'd as part of the salt of the earth,
    But he died years ago, very old.

143

'Twas his last sad request — so we laid him away
  In the trunk of an old hollow tree.
' Wake me up! ' was his charge, ' at the first break
    of day —
  Wake me up for the great jubilee!'
      The Good Time Coming is almost here!
      It was long, long, long on the way!
      Now run and tell Elijah to hurry up Pomp,
      And meet us at the gumtree down in the
        swamp,
      To wake Nicodemus to-day.''

While *Marching through Georgia* is, without doubt, Mr. Work's most renowned war song, his *Song of a Thousand Years* has about it a rise and swell, and a sublimity both in expression and melody, that surpasses anything else that he has written. The chorus is peculiarly fine both in words and music.

Work's songs brought him a considerable fortune. After the close of the war he made an extended tour through Europe, and while on the sea wrote a song which became very famous, entitled *The Ship that Never Returned.* During the later years of his life he wrote *Come Home, Father*, and *King Bibbler's Army* — both famous temperance songs.

After his return from Europe, Work invested his fortune in a fruit-growing enterprise in Vineland, New Jersey. He was also a somewhat remarkable inventor, and a patented knitting machine, a walking doll, and a rotary engine are among his numerous achievements. These years were saddened by financial and domestic misfortunes. His wife became insane, and died in an asylum in 1883. He survived her only a year, dying suddenly of heart disease on June 8, 1884, at Hartford, Connecticut. His ashes rest in Spring Grove Cemetery in that city, and on Decoration Day the Grand Army of the Republic never fail to strew flowers on the grave of the singer whose words and melodies led many an army to deeds of heroism. May a grateful people keep his memory green, and cause his grave to blossom for " A Thousand Years! "

JOHN WALLACE HUTCHINSON

TENTING ON THE OLD CAMP GROUND.

We're tenting to-night on the old camp ground;
  Give us a song to cheer
Our weary hearts, a song of home,
  And friends we love so dear.
      Many are the hearts that are weary to-night,
        Wishing for the war to cease,
      Many are the hearts, looking for the right,
        To see the dawn of peace.
      Tenting to-night, tenting to-night,
        Tenting on the old camp ground.

We've been tenting to-night on the old camp ground,
  Thinking of days gone by,
Of the loved ones at home, that gave us the hand,
  And the tear that said " Good-bye! "

We are tired of war on the old camp ground,
  Many are dead and gone,
Of the brave and true who've left their homes
  Others been wounded long.

We've been fighting to-day on the old camp ground,
  Many are lying near;
Some are dead, and some are dying,
  Many are in tears.
                        —*Walter Kittredge.*

Walter Kittredge was born in Merrimac, New Hampshire, October 8, 1832. His father was a farmer, and though New Hampshire farms are proverbial for their stony hillsides, they were fertile for the production of large families in those days, and Walter was the tenth of eleven children. His education was received at the village school. Like most other writers of war songs, Kittredge had an ear for music from the very first. All of his knowledge of music, however, he picked up for himself, as he never had an opportunity of attending music schools, or being under a teacher. He writes: "My father bought one of the first seraphines [a species of melodeon] made in Concord, New Hampshire, and well do I remember when the man came to put it up. To hear him play a simple melody was a rich treat, and this event was an important epoch in my child life."

Tenting on the Old Camp Ground, more than any other of our American war songs, had in it the heart experience of the man who wrote it. In 1863 Kittredge was drafted into the army. That night he went to bed the prey of many conflicting emotions. He was loyal to the heart's core, but was full of grief at the thought of leaving his home, and his rather poetic and timid nature revolted against war. In the middle of the night he awoke from a troubled sleep with the burden of dread still on his mind. In the solemnity and stillness of the

night the sad and pathetic fancies of the battle
field filled his thought. He reflected on how many
of the dear boys had already gone over to the un-
seen shore, killed in battle, or dead from disease in
the camps. He thought of the unknown graves, of
the sorrowful homes; of the weary waiting for the
end of the cruel strife, of the trials and hardships
of the tented field where the brave soldier boys
waited for the coming battle, which might be their
last. Suddenly these reflections began to take
form in his mind. ·He arose and began to write.
The first verse reveals his purpose not only to give
cheer to others, but to comfort his own heart: —

" We're tenting to-night on the old camp ground;
   Give us a song to cheer
  Our weary hearts, a song of home!
   And friends we loved so dear."

That verse was like a prayer to God for comfort and
the prayer was heard and answered.

Being a musician, a tune for the song easily came
to Kittredge's mind, and after copying both words
and music he went at once to Lynn, Massachusetts,
to visit his friend, Asa Hutchinson, one of the
famous Hutchinson family, who then lived at Bird's
Nest Cottage, at High Rock. After they had looked
it over together, they called in John Hutchinson,
who still lives, the "last of the Hutchinsons," to
sing the solo. Asa Hutchinson sang the bass, and

the children joined in the chorus. Kittredge at once made a contract with Asa Hutchinson to properly arrange and publish the song for one-half the profits.

The Hutchinson family were just then giving a series of torchlight concerts on the crest of old High Rock, with the tickets at the exceedingly popular price of five cents. The people from all the towns about turned out *en masse*. They had half a dozen or more ticket sellers and ·takers stationed at the various approaches to the rock. During the day they would wind balls of old cloth and soak them in oil. These, placed in pans on the top of posts at intervals, would burn quite steadily for an hour or more, and boys stood ready to replace them when they burned out. The audience gathered in thousands every night during this remarkable series of concerts, and on the very night of the day Kittredge had brought his new hymn, *Tenting on the Old Camp Ground* was sung for the first time from the crest of High Rock.

Like so many other afterward famous songs, it was hard to find a publisher at first, but the immense popularity which sprang up from the singing of the hymn about Boston soon led a Boston publisher to hire some one to write another song with a similar title, and a few weeks later the veteran music publisher, Ditson, brought out the original. Its sale reached many hundreds of thousands of copies during the war, and since then it has retained its popularity perhaps as completely as any of our war lyrics. It has been specially popular at reunions of soldiers, and every Grand Army assembly calls for it. Many a time I have seen the old veteran wiping away the tears as he listened to the singing of the second verse: —

" We've been tenting to-night on the old camp
     ground,
   Thinking of days gone by,
 Of the loved ones at home, that gave us the hand,
   And the tear that said ' Good-bye.' "

JULIA WARD HOWE

THE BATTLE HYMN OF THE REPUBLIC.

Mine eyes have seen the glory of the coming of the
  Lord;
He is trampling out the vintage where the grapes
  of wrath are stored;
He hath loosed the fatal lightning of his terrible
  swift sword:
  His truth is marching on.

I have seen him in the watchfires of a hundred cir-
  cling camps;
They have builded him an altar in the evening dews
  and damps;
I have read his righteous sentence by the dim and
  flaring lamps;
  His day is marching on.

I have read a fiery gospel writ in burnished rows of
  steel:
" As ye deal with my contemners, so with you my
  grace shall deal;
Let the Hero, born of woman, crush the serpent
  with his heel,
  Since God is marching on."

He has sounded forth the trumpet that shall never
call retreat;
He is sifting out the hearts of men before his
judgment-seat;
Oh, be swift, my soul, to answer him! be jubilant,
my feet!
Our God is marching on.

In the beauty of the lilies Christ was born across
the sea,
With a glory in his bosom that transfigures you and
me;
As he died to make men holy, let us die to make
men free,
While God is marching on.

—*Julia Ward Howe.*

This is, perhaps, the most elevated and lofty
strain of American patriotism. Julia Ward Howe
is a worthy author of such a hymn. She was the
daughter of Samuel Ward, a solid New York banker
of his time. Her mother, Julia Rush Ward, was
herself a poet of good ability. Mrs. Howe received
a very fine education, and, in addition to ordinary
college culture, speaks fluently Italian, French, and
Greek. In her girlhood she was a devout student
of Kant, Hegel, Spinoza, Comte, and Fichte. Her
literary work had given her considerable prominence
before her marriage to Dr. Samuel Gridley Howe,

of Boston, just then famous for his self-sacrificing services in association with Lord Byron in behalf of the liberty of the Greeks, and henceforth to become forever immortal for his life-long devotion to the cause of the blind. America never produced a more daring and benevolent man than Doctor Howe.

The *Battle Hymn of the Republic* had its birth-throes amid the storms of war. In December, 1861, Mrs. Howe, in company with her husband, Governor and Mrs. John A. Andrew, Rev. Dr. James Freeman Clarke, and other friends, made a journey to Washington. They arrived in the night. As their train sped on through the darkness, they saw in vivid contrast the camp fires of the pickets set to guard the line of the railroad. The troops lay encamped around the Capital City, their lines extending to a considerable distance. At the hotel where the Boston party were entertained, officers and their orderlies were conspicuous, and army ambulances were constantly arriving and departing. The gallop of horsemen, the tramp of foot soldiers, the noise of drum, fife, and bugle were heard continually. The two great powers were holding each other in check, and the very air seemed tense with expectancy. The one absorbing thought in Washington was the army, and the time of the visitors was generally employed in visits to the camps and hospitals.

One day during this visit a party which included

Doctor and Mrs. Howe and Doctor Clarke attended a review of the Union troops at a distance of several miles from the city. The maneuvers were interrupted by a sudden attack of the enemy, and instead of the spectacle promised them, they saw some reinforcements of cavalry gallop hastily to the aid of a small force of Federal troops which had been surprised and surrounded. They returned to the city as soon as possible, but their progress was much impeded by marching troops who nearly filled the highway. As they had to drive very slowly, in order to beguile the time they began to sing army songs, among which the John Brown song soon came to mind. This caught the ear of the soldiers and they joined in the inspiring chorus, and made it ring and ring again. Mrs. Howe was greatly impressed by the long lines of soldiers and the devotion and enthusiasm which they evinced, as they sung while they marched, *John Brown's Body.* James Freeman Clarke, seeing Mrs. Howe's deep emotion which was mirrored in her intense face, said:

" You ought to write some new words to go with that tune."

" I will," she earnestly replied.

She went back to Washington, went to bed, and finally fell asleep. She awoke in the night to find her now famous hymn beginning to form itself in her brain. As she lay still in the dark room, line

after line and verse after verse shaped themselves.
When she had thought out the last of these, she felt
that she dared not go to sleep again lest they should
be effaced by a morning nap. She sprang out of
bed and groped about in the dim December twilight
to find a bit of paper and the stump of a pencil with
which she had been writing the evening before.
Having found these articles, and having long been
accustomed to jot down stray thoughts with scarcely
any light in a room made dark for the repose of
her infant children, she very soon completed her
writing, went back to bed, and fell fast asleep.

What sublime and splendid words she had writ-
ten! There is in them the spirit of the old prophets.
Nothing could be grander than the first line: —

" Mine eyes have seen the glory of the coming of
the Lord."

In the second verse one sees through her eyes the
vivid picture she had witnessed in her afternoon's
visit to the army: —

" I have seen him in the watchfires of a hundred
circling camps;
They have builded him an altar in the evening
dews and damps;
I can read his righteous sentence by the dim and
flaring lamps;
His day is marching on."

In the third and fourth verses there is a triumphant note of daring faith and prophecy that was wonderfully contagious, and millions of men and women took heart again as they read or sang and caught its optimistic note: —

" He has sounded forth the trumpet that shall
   never call retreat;
 He is sifting out the hearts of men before his
   judgment-seat;
 Oh, be swift, my soul, to answer him! be jubilant,
   my feet!
      Our God is marching on. ''

On returning to Boston, Mrs. Howe carried her hymn to James T. Fields, at that time the editor of the *Atlantic Monthly*, and it was first published in that magazine. The title, *The Battle Hymn of the Republic*, was the work of Mr. Fields.

Strange to say, when it first appeared the song aroused no special attention. Though it was destined to have such world-wide appreciation, it won its first victory in Libby Prison. Nearly a year after its publication, a copy of a newspaper containing it was smuggled into the prison, where many hundreds of Northern officers and soldiers were confined, among them being the brilliant Chaplain, now Bishop, Charles C. McCabe. The Chaplain could sing anything and make music out of it, but he seized on this splendid battle hymn with enthusiastic delight. It makes the blood in one's veins boil again with patriotic fervor to hear him tell how the tears rained down strong men's cheeks as they sang in the Southern prison, far away from home and friends, those wonderful closing lines: —

" In the beauty of the lilies Christ was born across
  the sea,
 With a glory in his bosom that transfigures you
  and me;
 As he died to make men holy, let us die to make
  men free,
   While God is marching on."

It was Chaplain McCabe who had the privilege and honor of calling public attention to the song after his release. He came to Washington and in his lecture (that has come to be almost as famous as the battle hymn) on " The Bright Side of Life in Libby Prison," he described the singing of the hymn by himself and his companions in that dismal place of confinement. People now began to ask who had written the hymn, and the author's name was easily established by a reference to the magazine.

GEORGE FREDERICK ROOT

JUST BEFORE THE BATTLE, MOTHER.

Just before the battle, mother,
  I am thinking most of you,
While upon the field we're watching,
  With the enemy in view —
Comrades brave are round me lying,
  Fill'd with tho't of home and God;
For well they know that on the morrow,
  Some will sleep beneath the sod.
    Farewell, mother, you may never
    Press me to your heart again;
    But oh, you'll not forget me, mother,
    If I'm number'd with the slain.

Oh I long to see you, mother,
  And the loving ones at home,
But I'll never leave our banner
  Till in honor I can come.
Tell the traitors all around you
  That their cruel words, we know,
In ev'ry battle kill our soldiers
  By the help they give the foe.

Hark! I hear the bugles sounding,
  'Tis the signal for the fight,
Now may God protect us, mother,
  As he ever does the right.

And our bright and happy home so far away,
    And the tears they fill my eyes,
    Spite of all that I can do,
Tho' I try to cheer my comrades and be gay.
        Tramp, tramp, tramp, the boys are
           marching,
      Cheer up, comrades, they will come,
      And beneath the starry flag
      We will breathe the air again,
      Of the freeland in our own beloved home.

  "In the battle front we stood,
    When their fiercest charge they made,
And they swept us off a hundred men or more;
    But before we reached their lines,
    They were beaten back dismayed,
And we heard the cry of vict'ry o'er and o'er.

  "So within the prison cell,
    We are waiting for the day
That shall come to open wide the iron door,
    And the hollow eye grows bright,
    And the poor heart almost gay,
As we think of seeing home and friends once
  more."

To appreciate the pathos of that song one needs
to hear a company of Grand Army Veterans tell
about singing it in Andersonville or Libby Prisons.

FORTRESS MONROE

Just Before the Battle, Mother appealed to the tender side of those who remained at home, and made it a very popular song not only for public gatherings, but in drawing-rooms, and camps in the twilight of the evening. The sequel to it, *Just After the Battle*, was equally as popular and retains its popularity though a generation has passed away since it was written. It, too, has the vein of optimism in it which runs through all of Doctor Root's work. Perhaps that is one of the secrets of his great power over the human heart. While he makes us weep with the tenderness of the sentiment, there is always a rainbow on his cloud, a rainbow with promises of a brighter to-morrow. *Just After the Battle* has that rainbow in it, in the hope expressed by the singer that he shall still see his mother again in the old home: —

"Still upon the field of battle
   I am lying, mother dear,
With my wounded comrades waiting
   For the morning to appear.
Many sleep to waken never,
   In this world of strife and death,
And many more are faintly calling,
   With their feeble dying breath.

     Mother dear, your boy is wounded,
     And the night is drear with pain,
     But still I feel that I shall see you,
     And the dear old home again.

"Oh, the first great charge was fearful,
    And a thousand brave men fell,
Still, amid the dreadful carnage,
    I was safe from shot and shell.
So, amid the fatal shower,
    I had nearly pass'd the day,
When here the dreaded Minie struck me,
    And I sunk amid the fray.

"Oh, the glorious cheer of triumph,
    When the foeman turn'd and fled,
Leaving us the field of battle,
    Strewn with dying and with dead.
Oh, the torture and the anguish,
    That I could not follow on,
But here amid my fallen comrades,
    I must wait till morning's dawn.''

CHARLES CARROLL SAWYER

WHEN THIS CRUEL WAR IS OVER.

Dearest love, do you remember,
  When we last did meet,
How you told me that you lov'd me,
  Kneeling at my feet?
Oh! how proud you stood before me,
  In your suit of blue,
When you vow'd to me and country
  Ever to be true.

        Weeping, sad and lonely,
        Hopes and fears how vain!
        When this cruel war is over,
        Praying that we meet again!

When the summer breeze is sighing,
  Mournfully along;
Or when autumn leaves are falling,
  Sadly breathes the song.
Oft in dreams I see thee lying
  On the battle plain,
Lonely, wounded, even dying,
  Calling, but in vain.

If amid the din of battle
  Nobly you should fall,
Far away from those who love you,
  None to hear you call —

Who would whisper words of comfort
  Who would soothe your pain?
Ah! the many cruel fancies,
  Ever in my brain.

But our country call'd you, darling,
  Angels cheer your way;
While our nation's sons are fighting,
  We can only pray.
Nobly strike for God and liberty,
  Let all nations see
How we love the starry banner,
  Emblem of the free.

                    —*Charles Carroll Sawyer.*

Charles Carroll Sawyer was born in Mystic, Connecticut, in 1833. His father, Captain Joshua Sawyer, was an old-fashioned Yankee sea captain. The family moved to New York when Charles was quite young, and he obtained his education in that city. The poetic instinct was marked in his youth, and at the age of twelve he wrote several sonnets which attracted a good deal of attention among his acquaintances. At the breaking out of the war he began to write war songs, and in a few months was recognized everywhere as one of the most successful musical composers of the day. His most popular songs were *Who will Care for Mother Now?* *Mother would Comfort Me*, and the one we have

selected—*When this Cruel War is Over*. Each of
these three songs named reached a sale of over a
million copies before the close of the war, and were
sung in almost every mansion and farmhouse and
cabin from the Atlantic to the Pacific throughout
all the northern part of the Union, as well as in
every camp where soldiers waited for battle.

His song, *Mother would Comfort Me*, was sug-
gested, as indeed were most of his songs, by a war
incident. A soldier in one of the New York regi-
ments had been wounded and was taken prisoner
at Gettysburg. He was placed in a Southern hos-
pital, and when the doctor told him that nothing
more could be done for him, his dying words
were: "Mother would comfort me if she were
here." When Sawyer learned of the incident, he
wrote the song, the first verse of which runs as
follows:—

" Wounded and sorrowful, far from my home,
    Sick among strangers, uncared for, unknown;
    Even the birds that used sweetly to sing
    Are silent, and swiftly have taken the wing.
    No one but mother can cheer me to-day,
    No one for me could so fervently pray;
    None to console me, no kind friend is near—
    Mother would comfort me if she were here."

This song captured the country at once, and spread
its author's fame everywhere.

On another occasion a telegram came to a Brooklyn wife concerning her husband who was killed on the battlefield. The last words of the despatch read: "He was not afraid to die." Sawyer caught up that note in the telegram, and wrote his splendid song beginning,—

> "Like a true and faithful soldier
>   He obeyed our country's call;
> Vowing to protect its banner
>   Or in battle proudly fall:
> Noble, cheerful, brave and fearless,
>   When most needed, ever nigh,
> Always living as a Christian,
>   'He was not afraid to die.'"

Another of his greatest creations found its inspiration in a similar way. During one of the battles, among the many noble men that fell was a young man who had been the only support of an aged and invalid mother for years. Overhearing the doctor tell those who were near him that he could not live, he placed his hands across his forehead, and with a trembling voice said, while burning tears ran down his cheeks: "Who will care for mother, now?" Sawyer took up these words which voiced the generous heart of the dying youth, and made them the title and theme of one of his noblest songs. The first verse is full of pathos,—

" Why am I so weak and weary,
  See how faint my heated breath,
All around to me seems darkness,
  Tell me, comrades, is this death?
Ah! how well I know your answer;
  To my fate I meekly bow,
If you'll only tell me truly
  Who will care for mother now?"

At that time, when every community throughout
the North as well as the South had more than one
mother whose sole dependence for the future days
of weakness and old age was the strong arm of some
soldier boy at the front, this song struck a chord
that was very tender, and it was sung and whistled
and played in street and theater and drawing-room
throughout the entire country.

Sawyer's songs were unique in that they were
popular in both armies. They never contained a
word of malice, and appealed to the universal hu-
man heart. At the close of the war a newspaper
published at Milledgeville, Georgia, said of Sawyer's
songs, " His sentiments are fraught with the great-
est tenderness, and never one word has he written
about the South or the war that could wound the
sore chords of a Southern heart."

The most universally famous of all Sawyer's
songs was *When this Cruel War is Over*. As the
long years of carnage dragged on, the fascination

for the glamour and glory of war disappeared, and
its horrid cruelty impressed people, North and
South, more and more. Loving hearts in the army
and at home caught up this song as an appropriate
expression of the hunger for peace that was in their
souls. A popular Southern song, *When upon the
Field of Glory*, the words of which were written
by J. H. Hewitt and the music by H. L. Schreiner,
was an answer to this song of Sawyer's. As it is
one of the best of the songs of the Confederacy, it
is worth repetition here:—

" When upon the field of glory,
   'Mid the battle cry,
And the smoke of cannon curling
   Round the mountain high;
Then sweet mem'ries will come o'er me,
   Painting home and thee,
Nerving me to deeds of daring,
   Struggling to be free.
      Weep no longer, dearest,
      Tears are now in vain.
      When this cruel war is over
      We may meet again.

" Oft I think of joys departed,
   Oft I think of thee;
When night's sisters throw around me,
   Their star'd canopy.

Dreams so dear come o'er my pillow,
　　Bringing up the past,
Oh! how sweet the soldier's visions!
　　Oh! how short they last!

" When I stand a lonely picket,
　　Gazing on the moon,
As she walks her starry pathway,
　　In night's silent noon;
I will think that thou art looking
　　On her placid face,
Then our tho'ts will meet together,
　　In a heav'nly place.

" When the bullet, swiftly flying
　　Thro' the murky air,
Hits its mark, my sorrow'd bosom,
　　Leaving death's pang there;
Then my tho'ts on thee will turn, love,
　　While I prostrate lie.
My pale lips shall breathe, 'God bless thee —
　　For our cause I die!'
　　　　Weep then for me, dearest,
　　　　When I'm free from pain;
　　　　When this cruel war is over,
　　　　In heav'n we'll meet again."

WILLIAM TECUMSEH SHERMAN

MARCHING THROUGH GEORGIA.

Bring the good old bugle, boys, we'll sing another
    song,
Sing it with a spirit that will start the world
    along,
Sing it as we used to sing it fifty thousand strong,
      While we were marching through Georgia.
      Hurrah! hurrah! We bring the jubilee!
      Hurrah! hurrah! The flag that makes you free!
      So we sang the chorus from Atlanta to the sea,
      While we were marching through Georgia.

How the darkies shouted when they heard the joyful
    sound!
How the turkeys gobbled which our commissary
    found!
How the sweet potatoes even started from the
    ground,
      While we were marching through Georgia.

Yes, and there were Union men who wept with joy-
    ful tears,
When they saw the honored flag they had not seen
    for years,
Hardly could they be restrained from breaking forth
    in cheers,
      While we were marching through Georgia.

193

" Sherman's dashing Yankee boys will never reach
    the coast! ''
So the saucy rebels said, and 'twas a handsome boast,
Had they not forgot, alas! to reckon with the host,
    While we were marching through Georgia.

So we made a thoroughfare for Freedom and her
    train,
Sixty miles in latitude; three hundred to the main;
Treason fled before us, for resistance was in vain,
    While we were marching through Georgia.

                —*Henry Clay Work.*

Among Mr. Work's famous war songs, none have
captured so wide an audience, or held their own so
well since the war, as *Marching through Georgia.*
I think it is the foraging idea, so happily expressed,
that, more than anything else except the contagious
music which starts the most rheumatic foot to keep-
ing time, has given this song its popular sway.
There was something so reckless and romantic in
Sherman's cutting loose from his base of supplies
and depending on the country through which he
marched for food for his army, that the song which
expressed this seized the imagination of the people.
    General Sherman in his *Memoirs* says: " The
skill and success of the men in collecting forage was
one of the features of this march. Each brigade
commander had authority to detail a company of

foragers, usually about fifty men with one or two commissioned officers, selected for their boldness and enterprise. This party would be despatched before daylight with a knowledge of the intended day's march and camp, would proceed on foot five or six miles from the route traveled by their brigade, and then visit every plantation and farm within range. They would usually procure a wagon, or family carriage, load it with bacon, cornmeal, turkeys, chickens, ducks, and everything that could be used as food or forage, and would then regain the main road, usually in advance of their train. When this came up, they would deliver to the brigade commissary the supplies thus gathered by the way. Often would I pass these foraging parties at the roadside, waiting for their wagons to come up, and was amused at their strange collections — mules, horses, even cattle, packed with old saddles and loaded with hams, bacon, bags of cornmeal, and poultry of every character and description. Although this foraging was attended with great danger and hard work, there seemed to be a charm about it that attracted the soldiers, and it was a privilege to be detailed on such a party. Daily they returned mounted on all sorts of beasts, which were at once taken from them and appropriated to the general use; but the next day they would start out again on foot, only to repeat the experience of the day before."

Bishop Ames, of the Methodist Episcopal Church,

used to greatly enjoy relating how he was invited
to share the carriage of a German Baron on the
occasion of the great military review in Washington
at the close of the war. They had a favorable
position for viewing the procession. Hour after
hour the soldiers marched by. There rumbled the
field artillery; there crowded by, with dripping
sides and champing mouths, the cavalry, and after
them tramped the unwearying infantry. At one
time there passed a brigade clothed in brand-new
uniforms, specially brought out for the occasion.
Every uniform was clean and beautiful, every
bayonet and sword polished and gleaming. The
drill was perfect. The men were at the highest
point of condition. Every motion and look bespoke
the well-drilled soldier. As they marched by the
Baron turned around excitedly to Bishop Ames and
said, "Pishop, those men can whip the world."

Immediately following them, purposely to bring
out the strong contrast, was a brigade of old veter-
ans, just as they came from their long campaign in
the South. They were some of the men who had
marched with Sherman to the sea — the men who
had picked up the ducks and the cornmeal by the
wayside. They were soiled and ragged. One man
had one leg of his trousers patched out by strange
cloth; another had no coat; another had a teakettle
swung on his gun over his shoulder; another had
part of a ham on his bayonet. So they represented

SHERMAN BURNS ATLANTA AND MARCHES TOWARD THE SEA

the march through Georgia. They rolled along with an easy, swinging gait, chatting, laughing, occasionally imitating some animal, giving a bark, or a howl, or a screech, yet every man a soldier and keeping step to the music and in line. As these men with their tattered uniforms and torn and stained flags went by, the Baron sprang up, and with tears rolling down his cheeks, threw his arms around Bishop Ames and cried: "Mein Gott! Pishop, these men could *whip the devil!*"

General Sherman himself was never enthusiastic over the song that has immortalized his famous march. I have been unable to find in his *Memoirs* a single reference to it; but he quotes there in full a fine song by Adjutant S. H. M. Byers which he evidently would have been very glad to have had replace the simpler lines of Mr. Work. But Work had the key to the people's heart, and his song will live as long as the American flag. Mr. Byers' song, however, is a splendid piece of work and well worth repeating here. General Sherman says that on the afternoon of February 17, 1865, on overhauling his pockets, according to custom, to read more carefully the various notes and memoranda received during the day, he found a paper which had been given him by a Union prisoner who had escaped from Columbia. " It proved," writes the General, "to be the song of *Sherman's March to the Sea*, which had been composed by Adjutant S. H. M.

Byers, of the Fifth Iowa Infantry, when a prisoner
in the asylum at Columbia, which had been beauti-
fully written off by a fellow-prisoner, and handed
to me in person. This appeared to me so good that
I at once sent for Byers, attached him to my staff,
provided him with horse and equipment, and took
him as far as Fayetteville, North Carolina, whence
he was sent to Washington as bearer of despatches."

The writing of this song was a good thing for
Byers, as it secured him the lifelong friendship of
General Sherman, and through his kindly support
he was afterward made consul at Zurich, Switzer-
land. Adjutant Byers said that there was among
the prisoners at Columbia an excellent glee club
who used to sing it well, with an audience, often,
of rebel ladies. It is truly a fine poem:—

"Our camp-fires shone bright on the mountain
    That frowned on the river below,
As we stood by our guns in the morning,
    And eagerly watched for the foe;
When a rider came out of the darkness
    That hung over mountain and tree,
And shouted, ' Boys, up and be ready!
    For Sherman will march to the sea!'
        Then sang we the song of our chieftain,
            That echoed over river and lea;
        And the stars in our banner shone brighter
            When Sherman marched down to the sea!

"Then cheer upon cheer for bold Sherman
   Went up from each valley and glen,
And the bugles reëchoed the music
   That came from the lips of the men;
For we knew that the stars in our banner
   More bright in their splendor would be,
And that blessings from Northland would greet us,
   When Sherman marched down to the sea!

"Then forward, boys! forward to battle!
   We marched on our wearisome way,
We stormed the wild hills of Resaca —
   God bless those who fell on that day!
Then Kenesaw frowned in its glory,
   Frowned down on the flag of the free;
But the East and the West bore our standard,
   And Sherman marched on to the sea!

"Still onward we pressed, till our banners
   Swept out from Atlanta's grim walls,
And the blood of the patriot dampened
   The soil where the traitor-flag falls;
But we paused not to weep for the fallen,
   Who slept by each river and tree,
Yet we twined a wreath of the laurel
   As Sherman marched down to the sea!

"Oh, proud was our army that morning,
   That stood where the pine darkly towers,
When Sherman said, ' Boys, you are weary,
   But to-day fair Savannah is ours!'

Then sang we the song of our chieftain,
   That echoed over river and lea;
And the stars in our banner shone brighter
   When Sherman camped down by the sea! ''

Plymouth Rock

ROBERT EDWARD LEE

MY MARYLAND.

The despot's heel is on thy shore,
    Maryland!
His torch is at thy temple door,
    Maryland!
Avenge the patriotic gore
That flecked the streets of Baltimore,
And be the battle queen of yore,
    Maryland, my Maryland!

Hark to an exiled son's appeal,
    Maryland!
My mother State, to thee I kneel,
    Maryland!
For life or death, for woe or weal,
Thy peerless chivalry reveal,
And gird thy beauteous limbs with steel,
    Maryland, my Maryland!

Thou wilt not cower in the dust,
    Maryland!
Thy beaming sword shall never rust,
    Maryland!
Remember Carroll's sacred trust,
Remember Howard's warlike thrust,
And all thy slumberers with the just,
    Maryland, my Maryland!

Come! 'Tis the red dawn of the day,
    Maryland!
Come with thy panoplied array,
    Maryland!
With Ringgold's spirit for the fray,
With Watson's blood at Monterey,
With fearless Lowe and dashing May,
    Maryland, my Maryland!

Dear mother, burst the tyrant's chain,
    Maryland!
Virginia should not call in vain,
    Maryland!
She meets her sisters on the plain,
"*Sic semper!*" 'tis the proud refrain
That baffles minions back amain,
    Maryland!
Arise in majesty again,
    Maryland, my Maryland!

Come! for thy shield is bright and strong,
    Maryland!
Come! for thy dalliance does thee wrong,
    Maryland!
Come to thine own heroic throng
Stalking with liberty along,
And chant thy dauntless slogan-song,
    Maryland, my Maryland!

I see the blush upon thy cheek,
    Maryland!
But thou wast ever bravely meek,
    Maryland!
But lo! There surges forth a shriek,
From hill to hill, from creek to creek,
Potomac calls to Chesapeake,
    Maryland, my Maryland!

Thou wilt not yield the Vandal toll,
    Maryland!
Thou wilt not crook to his control,
    Maryland!
Better the fire upon thee roll,
Better the shot, the blade, the bowl,
Than crucifixion of the soul,
    Maryland, my Maryland!

I hear the distant thunder-hum,
    Maryland!
The " Old Line's " bugle, fife, and drum,
    Maryland!
She is not dead, nor deaf, nor dumb;
Huzza! she spurns the Northern scum —
She breathes, she burns! She'll come!
  She'll come!
    Maryland, my Maryland!

            —James Ryder Randall.

My Maryland, one of the most popular songs

of the Confederacy, was written by James Ryder Randall, in 1861. Randall was at that time professor of English literature at Poydras College, upon the Fausse Rivière, of Louisiana. He was very young, and had but recently come from college in Maryland. He was full of poetry and romance, and when one day in April, 1861, he read in the New Orleans *Delta* the news of the attack on the Massachusetts Sixth as they passed through Baltimore, it fired his blood. " This account excited me greatly," Mr. Randall writes. " I had long been absent from my native city, and the startling event there inflamed my mind. That night I could not sleep, for my nerves were all unstrung, and I could not dismiss what I had read in the paper from my mind. About midnight I arose, lit a candle, and went to my desk. Some powerful spirit appeared to possess me, and almost involuntarily I proceeded to write the song of *My Maryland*. I remember that the idea appeared to take shape first as music in the brain — some wild air that I cannot now recall. The whole poem of nine stanzas, as originally written, was dashed off rapidly when once begun."

As Doctor Matthews well says, there is often a feeling afloat in the minds of men, undefined and vague for want of one to give it form, and held in solution, as it were, until a chance word dropped in the ear of a poet suddenly crystallizes this feeling into song, in which all may see clearly and sharply

THE INVASION OF MARYLAND
(View from Maryland Heights)

reflected what in their own thought was shapeless and hazy. It was young Randall's fortune to be the instrument through which the South spoke, and, by a natural reaction, his burning lines helped " fire the Southern heart."

The form of the poem was suggested by Mangan's *Karamanian Exile,*—

> " I see thee ever in my dreams,
> > Karaman!
> > Thy hundred hills, thy thousand streams,
> > > Karaman, O Karaman!
> > As when thy gold-bright morning gleams,
> > As when the deepening sunset seams
> > With lines of light thy hills and streams,
> > > Karaman!
> > So now thou loomest on my dreams,
> > > Karaman, O Karaman!"

The previous use of this form, which is perhaps the most effective possible for a battle hymn, by no means detracts from Randall's stirring poem.

The poem would never have had great effect, however, if it had not been fortunate in drafting to its service a splendid piece of music. Miss Hattie Cary, of Baltimore, afterward the wife of Professor H. M. Martin, of Johns-Hopkins University, brought about the wedding which enabled Randall's song to reach every camp-fire of the Southern armies. " The Glee Club was to hold its meeting

in our parlors one evening early in June," she
writes, "and my sister Jennie, being the only
musical member of the family, had charge of the
program on the occasion. With a schoolgirl's
eagerness to score a success, she resolved to secure
some new and ardent expression of feelings that
were by this time wrought up to the point of explo-
sion. In vain she searched through her stock of
songs and airs — nothing seemed intense enough
to suit her. Aroused by her tone of despair, I
came to the rescue with the suggestion that she
should adapt the words of *Maryland, my Mary-
land*, which had been constantly on my lips since
the appearance of the lyric a few days before in the
South. I produced the paper and began declaim-
ing the verses. '*Lauriger Horatius*,' she exclaimed,
and in a flash the immortal song found a voice in
the stirring air so perfectly adapted to it. That
night when her contralto voice rang out the stanzas,
the refrain rolled forth from every throat without
pause or preparation; and the enthusiasm com-
municated itself with such effect to the crowd
assembled beneath our windows as to endanger
seriously the liberties of the party."

This air was originally an old German student
melody used for a lovely German lyric, *Tannen-
baum, O Tannenbaum*, which Longfellow has num-
bered among his translations. The first verse is as
follows, —

" O hemlock tree! O hemlock tree! how faithful are
  thy branches!
 Green not only in summer time,
 But in the winter's frost and rime!
 O hemlock tree! O hemlock tree! how faithful are
  thy branches! "

Some one has well said that the transmigration of
tunes is a large and fertile subject. The capturing
of the air of a jolly college song and harnessing it
to the service of a fiery battle hymn may seem very
strange, but not so to those who are familiar with
the adventures which a tune has often undergone.

This song was not only popular through the
South, but so stately and pleasing was the melody
that it was often sung in the North. A soldier
relates: " I remember hearing it sung under circum-
stances that for the time made me fancy it was the
sweetest song I ever listened to. Our command
had just reached Frederick City, Maryland, after a
distressing forced march, and going into bivouac,
the staff to which I was attached took up their
quarters on the piazza of a lonely mansion, and
there, wrapping themselves in their blankets, with
their saddles for pillows, sought needed repose.
Sleep would not come to my eyelids. The night
was a delicious one; it was warm, but a slight
breeze was stirring, and the sky was clear, and the
stars shone brilliantly. The stillness was profound,

every one around me was asleep, when suddenly there fell upon my ears the song:—

> ' The despot's heel is on thy shore,
> Maryland! '

The voice was a mezzo-soprano, full, round, and clear, and the charming melody was sung with infinite tenderness and delicacy of shading. I listened almost breathlessly, for it was the first time I had heard the song, and as it was ended, I arose for the purpose of ascertaining who it was that sang so sweetly. I found her in the person of a plump negro girl of about sixteen years, with a face blacker than the smoke in Vulcan's smithy.''

A delightful contrast to the attack of the mob on the Massachusetts Sixth, in Baltimore, in 1861, was furnished recently when the historic Sixth from Boston passed through Baltimore on their way to the South to take part in the invasion of Cuba. Baltimore gave herself up to seeing how splendidly she could receive the regiment that had once been mobbed in her streets. They were received at the station by the Mayor, the school-children were drawn up in line along the route of march, and the soldiers from Massachusetts were pelted with flowers instead of stones and bullets. Each soldier was given a little box containing cake and fruit, and a love letter, while a great motto met their eyes which said: '' Let the welcome of '98 efface the memory of '61.''

ULYSSES SIMPSON GRANT

ALL QUIET ALONG THE POTOMAC.

" All quiet along the Potomac," they say,
  " Except now and then a stray picket
Is shot, as he walks on his beat, to and fro,
  By a rifleman hid in the thicket.
'Tis nothing: a private or two now and then
  Will not count in the news of the battle;
Not an officer lost, only one of the men
  Moaning out all alone the death-rattle."

All quiet along the Potomac to-night,
  Where the soldiers lie peacefully dreaming;
Their tents in the rays of the clear autumn moon,
  Or the light of the watchfires, are gleaming.
A tremulous sigh, as the gentle night-wind
  Through the forest leaves softly is creeping:
While stars up above, with their glittering eyes,
  Keep guard,— for the army is sleeping.

There's only the sound of the lone sentry's tread,
  As he tramps from the rock to the fountain,
And thinks of the two in the low trundle-bed,
  Far away in the cot on the mountain.
His musket falls slack, his face, dark and grim,
  Grows gentle with memories tender,
As he mutters a prayer for the children asleep;
  For their mother — may heaven defend her!

The moon seems to shine just as brightly as then,
  That night when the love yet unspoken
Leaped up to his lips, when low, murmured vows
  Were pledged to be ever unbroken;
Then drawing his sleeve roughly over his eyes,
  He dashes off tears that are welling,
And gathers his gun closer up to his side,
  As if to keep down the heart swelling.

He passes the fountain, the blasted pine tree,
  The footstep is lagging and weary,
Yet onward he goes, through the broad belt of
    light,
  Toward the shade of the forest so dreary.
Hark! was it the night-wind that rustled the
    leaves,
  Was it moonlight so wondrously flashing?
It looked like a rifle —" Ha! Mary, good-bye,"
  And the lifeblood is ebbing and plashing.

All quiet along the Potomac to-night,
  No sound save the rush of the river;
While soft falls the dew on the face of the dead,
  The picket's off duty forever.
Hark! was it the night-wind that rustled the
    leaves,
  Was it moonlight so wondrously flashing?
It looked like a rifle —" Ha! Mary, good-bye,"
  And the lifeblood is ebbing and plashing.

                  —Ethel Lynn Beers.

Mrs. Beers's right to the authorship of this famous song has been very severely contested, but there seems to be no reason now to doubt that the really fine poem is hers. Though there have been numerous claimants for its authorship, the one who has come nearest to carrying the day is, strange to say, a Southerner. It is curious indeed that a war song should be claimed by both sides, but that has been the story of this song. This Southerner is Lamar Fontaine. Mr. Fontaine was born at Gay Hill, Texas. Twenty years before the war his father moved to Austin, Texas, and was secretary to General Lamar, for whom the son was named. When the war broke out this young Lamar Fontaine became a major in the Confederate Army. Some time in 1862, when the poem *All Quiet Along the Potomac* appeared in a Southern newspaper, Lamar Fontaine's name was attached to it. Davidson, the author of *Living Writers of the South*, wrote to Fontaine in regard to the authorship of this hymn, and in replying Fontaine said: "The poem in question was written by me while our army lay at Fairfax Courthouse, or rather the greater portion, in and around that place. On the second day of August, 1861, I first read it to a few of my messmates in Company I, Second Virginia Cavalry. During the month of August I gave away many manuscript copies to soldiers, and some few to ladies in and about Leesburg, Loudon County,

Virginia. In fact, I think that most of the men belonging to the Second Virginia, then commanded by Colonel Radford, were aware of the fact that I was the author of it. I never saw the piece in print until just before the battle of Leesburg (October 21, 1861), and then it was in a Northern paper with the notice that it had been found on the dead body of a picket. I hope the controversy between myself and others in regard to *All Quiet Along the Potomac To-night*, will soon be forever settled. I wrote it, and the world knows it; and they may howl over it, and give it to as many authors as they please. I wrote it, and I am a Southern man, and I am proud of the title, and am glad that my children will know that the South was the birthplace of their fathers, from their generation back to the seventh."

Another Southern man, however, and a distinguished one, puts a very different look on the case. Mr. Chandler Harris of Georgia writes a letter for insertion in Mr. Davidson's volume in the course of which he says: "After a careful and impartial investigation of all the facts in my reach, I have come to the conclusion that Mrs. Beers, and not Mr. Fontaine, wrote the poem in question. My reasons for believing that Mr. Fontaine is not the author of *All Quiet*, are several:

"1. The poem appeared in *Harper's Weekly* for November 30, 1861, as *The Picket Guard*, over the initials of Mrs. Ethel Beers of New York.

MOUNT VERNON

" 2. It did not make its appearance in any Southern paper until about April or May, 1862.

" 3. It was published as having been found in the pocket of a dead soldier on the battlefield. It is more than probable that the dead soldier was a Federal, and that the poem had been clipped from *Harper's*.

" 4. I have compared the poem in *Harper's* with the same as it first appeared in the Southern papers, and find the punctuation to be precisely the same.

" 5. Mr. Fontaine, so far as I have seen, has given elsewhere no evidence of the powers displayed in that poem. I, however, remember noticing in the Charleston *Courier*, in 1863, or 1864, a ' Parodie' (as Mr. L. F. had it) on Mrs. Norton's *Bingen on the Rhine*, which was positively the poorest affair I ever saw. Mr. Fontaine had just come out of a Federal prison, and some irresponsible editor, in speaking of this ' Parodie' remarked that the poet's Pegasus had probably worn his wings out against the walls of his Northern dungeon.

" You probably know me well enough to acquit me, in this instance at least, of the charge of prejudice. I am jealous of Southern literature, and if I have any partiality in the matter at all, it is in favor of Major Lamar Fontaine's claim. I should like to claim this poem for that gentleman; I should be glad to claim it as a specimen of Southern literature, but the facts in the case do not warrant it."

Mr. Alfred H. Guernsey, for many years editor of *Harper's Magazine*, bears testimony that the poem, bearing the title *The Picket Guard*, appeared in *Harper's Weekly* for November 30, 1861.. He further declares that it was furnished by Mrs. Ethel Lynn Beers, whom he describes as " a lady whom I think incapable of palming off as her own any production of another."

Mrs. Beers was born in Goshen, New York, and her maiden name was Ethelinda Eliot. She was a direct descendant of John Eliot, the heroic apostle to the Indians. When she began to write for the newspapers she signed her contributions " Ethel Lynn," a *nom de plume* very naturally suggested by her Christian name. After her marriage, she added her husband's name, and over the signature of Ethel Lynn Beers published many poems. In her later years Mrs. Beers resided in Orange, New Jersey, where she died October 10, 1879, on the very day on which her poems, among them *All Quiet Along the Potomac*, were issued in book form.

There has never been any contest as to the music of the song, which was composed by J. Dayton, the leader of the band of the First Connecticut Artillery.

STEPHEN COLLINS FOSTER

THE OLD FOLKS AT HOME.

Way down upon de Suwanee ribber,
    Far, far away,
Dere's wha my heart is turning ebber,
    Dere's wha de old folks stay.
All up and down de whole creation,
    Sadly I roam,
Still longin' for de old plantation,
    And for de old folks at home.
        All de world am sad and dreary,
            Eb'rywhere I roam.
        Oh! darkies, how my heart grows
            weary,
        Far from de old folks at home.

All round de little farm I wander'd
    When I was young,
Den many happy days I squander'd,
    Many de songs I sung.
When I was playin' wid my brudder,
    Happy was I,
Oh! take me to my kind old mudder,
    Dere let me live and die.

One little hut among de bushes,
    One dat I love,
Still sadly to my mem'ry rushes,
    No matter where I rove.

When will I see de bees a-humming
All round de comb?
When will I hear de banjo tumming
Down in my good old home?

—*Stephen Collins Foster*.

Stephen Collins Foster has a very tender place in the hearts of the American people. His songs are marked by a tenderness and pathos which goes straight to the fountain of tears. Foster was born on the 4th of July, 1826, at Lawrenceburg, Pennsylvania. His native town was founded by his father, but was many years ago merged into the city of Pittsburg.

Young Foster had good opportunities for education in an academy at Allegheny, Pennsylvania, and afterward at Jefferson College. He had a genius for music almost from his birth; while yet but a baby he could wake sweet harmonies from any musical instrument he touched. At the age of seven he had mastered the flageolet without a teacher, and had already become quite proficient on the piano and the flute. He had a clear though not a very strong voice, but one that was under perfect control. As a lad he wrote his first composition, a waltz, which was rendered at a school commencement. The composition, coming from so young a boy, attracted a good deal of attention. His talent for music was so marked that he became the leader throughout his school days of all musical affairs among the students, and he was the center of every serenading party or concert. To compose the words and music of a song was his chief delight. He wrote the words first, and then hummed them over and over till he found notes that would express them properly. While he was in the academy a minstrel troupe came to town and he attended their performance. He succeeded in having one of his songs introduced into their program the next night, which greatly pleased the local public. This was *Oh, Susanna*, which was afterward published in 1842, and immediately gained great popularity. This aroused his musical enthusiasm, and he offered still other songs to publishers, and finally determined to devote himself to musical composition for a livelihood. He attended all the negro camp meetings he could reach, listened to the songs of colored people, gathering new ideas, and this faithful reproduction of what was up to that time an undiscovered mine of musical possibilities, was the secret of his great success as a writer of negro melodies.

Foster had a deeply poetic soul, and would go into the wildest ecstasy over a pretty melody or a bit of rich harmony. There is a certain vein of tender retrospect in nearly all his songs. Take *Old Dog Tray*, of which a hundred and twenty-five thousand copies were sold the first eighteen months after publication. There is something exceedingly tender about it:—

" The morn of life is past, and ev'ning comes at last,
   It brings me a dream of a once happy day,
Of merry forms I've seen upon the village green,
   Sporting with my old dog Tray.
        Old dog Tray's ever faithful,
        Grief cannot drive him away,
        He's gentle, he is kind; I'll never, never
          find
        A better friend than Old Dog Tray! "

How often we say one to another, " It is good to be missed." But no one has ever voiced that universal feeling of the heart as perfectly as has Foster in his popular song, *Do They Miss Me at Home?*

" Do they miss me at home, do they miss me?
   'Twould be an assurance most dear,
To know that this moment some lov'd one
   Were saying, ' I wish he were here;
To feel that the group at the fireside
   Were thinking of me as I roam;
Oh, yes, 'twould be joy beyond measure
   To know that they miss me at home. "

Foster was a most prolific writer, producing between two and three hundred popular songs, furnishing both the words and the music. Among his best known war songs are *We've a Million in the*

Field, Stand by the Flag, For the Dear Old Flag I Die, and *Was my Brother in the Battle?* His most famous song, however, and one which he hoped would rival *Home, Sweet Home,*—a song of which the soldiers amid the loneliness and homesickness of camp never grew weary — was *The Old Folks at Home.* For the time it has been before the public, it is probably the best known song in the world. Four hundred thousand copies of it were sold the first few years after it was written. The tune has crossed all oceans and become a favorite with martial bands of music in every region of the earth.

The author of this sweet old melody that touches the heart of all peoples closed his life in great sorrow and poverty. In the days of his youth and early manhood he was greatly beloved by all who knew him. He had multitudes of friends and in character was modest, unassuming, and almost as shy as a girl. He was happily married in 1854, in Pittsburg, but the bright prospects which he then had of a happy home life were eclipsed through his yielding to the appetite for strong drink. In 1860 his dissipation separated him from his family, and he settled in New York City, where for awhile he kept an old down-town grocery on the corner of Hester and Christy Streets. Some of his most famous songs were composed in the back room of that old grocery on pieces of brown wrapping-paper. Many of these songs that under the impelling force of his appetite for drink were sold for a few dollars, often brought hundreds and even thousands of dollars to the purchasers.

On the 12th of January, 1864, he was injured by a fall, and died on the following day in Bellevue Hospital, friendless, and in abject poverty. This brilliant man whose melodies were sung by hundreds and thousands of tongues, and to whom a single publisher had paid more than twenty thousand dollars of royalties on his music, died lonely in a great city, and his body was carried back to his native State through the charity of the Pennsylvania Railroad Company. His funeral, however, was attended by an immense concourse of people, comprising both the rich and poor of Pittsburg who remembered his brighter days, and who felt that the city was honored by his genius. Musicians attended in large force, and the songs they sang above his grave were his own melodies.

FRANCIS MILES FINCH

THE BLUE AND THE GRAY. ₙₑₜ

By the flow of the inland river,
  Whence the fleets of iron have fled,
Where the blades of the grave-grass quiver,
  Asleep are the ranks of the dead;
    Under the sod and the dew,
      Waiting the judgment day;
    Under the one the Blue;
      Under the other the Gray.

These, in the robings of glory;
  Those, in the gloom of defeat;
All, with the battle-blood gory,
  In the dusk of eternity meet;
    Under the sod and the dew,
      Waiting the judgment day;
    Under the laurel, the Blue;
      Under the willow, the Gray.

From the silence of sorrowful hours
  The desolate mourners go,
Lovingly laden with flowers
  Alike for the friend and foe;
    Under the sod and the dew,
      Waiting the judgment day;
    Under the roses, the Blue;
      Under the lilies, the Gray.

So, with an equal splendor,
  The morning sun-rays fall,
With a touch impartially tender,
  On the blossoms blooming for all;
    Under the sod and the dew,
      Waiting the judgment day;
    Broidered with gold, the Blue;
      Mellowed with gold, the Gray.

So when the summer calleth
  On forest and field of grain,
With an equal murmur falleth
  The cooling drip of the rain;
    Under the sod and the dew,
      Waiting the judgment day;
    Wet with the rain, the Blue;
      Wet with the rain, the Gray.

Sadly, but not with upbraiding,
  The generous deed was done;
In the storm of the years that are fading,
  No braver battle was won;
    Under the sod and the dew,
      Waiting the judgment day;
    Under the blossoms, the Blue;
      Under the garlands, the Gray.

No more shall the war cry sever.
  Or the winding rivers be red;
They banish our anger forever,
  When they laurel the graves of our dead!

> Under the sod and the dew.
> Waiting the judgment day;
> Love and tears for the Blue;
> Tears and love for the Gray.
>
> —*Francis Miles Finch.*

Francis Miles Finch, the author of *The Blue and the Gray*, was born in Ithaca, New York, in 1827. He graduated with honor from Yale College in 1845, in his eighteenth year. He studied law and became a practicing lawyer of fine reputation at Ithaca, being elected an associate judge of the Court of Appeals of the State of New York in 1881. In July, 1853, he read a poem at the centennial celebration of the Linonian Society of Yale, in which several lyrics were introduced, including one on Nathan Hale, the patriot spy of the Revolution. This at once achieved wide popularity. His one poem, however, which will carry his name down to the future is *The Blue and the Gray*.

Two years after the war of the Rebellion there appeared in the New York *Tribune*, the following item: "The women of Columbus, Mississippi, animated by nobler sentiments than many of their sisters, have shown themselves impartial in their offerings made to the memory of the dead. They strewed flowers alike on the graves of the Confederate and of the National soldiers." This, coming at a time when a great deal of the soreness of defeat and the bitterness aroused by the war still remained, seemed to be the first indication of an era of more kindly feeling and a more generous Christian spirit.

The eye of a poet is always seeing the poetic possibilities in current incidents, and when Mr. Finch saw this news item in his favorite daily paper, he not only saw the romance and pathos of the situation, but thought that such an exhibition of generosity should be at once met and welcomed in the same temper. It was out of that impulse that *The Blue and the Gray* grew into being. Mr. Finch sent it to the *Atlantic Monthly*, where it was published in the September number of 1867, prefaced with the news extract from the *Tribune* which had suggested it. The poem at once aroused marked attention and became popular throughout the entire country, but especially so in the South.

John Hutchinson was paying a visit to Vinnie Ream, the sculptor, who designed the General Thomas monument in April, 1874. Among the guests were three ex-Confederate generals. At her request Hutchinson sang *The Blue and the Gray;* when he had finished singing the song, the three Confederates rose simultaneously, and one after the other shook his hand with great heartiness. "Mr. Hutchinson," they said, "that song is a passport to you anywhere in the South." Alexander H. Stephens, the ex-vice-president of the Confederacy, upon hearing from these gentlemen of Mr. Hutchinson's

GRANT'S MONUMENT

singing, sent a special request to him to come to his hotel and sing *The Blue and the Gray*. He was wheeled into the room in his chair to listen to the song. At the conclusion he declared that the country was safe when such sentiments became popular.

Mr. Hutchinson himself composed the music for Finch's famous song. At the great Atlanta Exposition in 1895, Mr. Hutchinson made the journey to Atlanta by special invitation of the management, and was present on "Blue and Gray" Day. He says of the experience: "Who can picture my thoughts on that notable occasion? To think that, at last, the man who had known what it was to be maligned and buffeted in the South, should be received with honor in its chief city, and witness the effects of reconstruction in the great cotton country! It was a 'New South,' indeed, that I saw. And there, to the great gathering of Union and Confederate soldiers, I sang the song that had so often in later years been a key to open the Southern heart to the Hutchinsons: —

> " ' No more shall the war cry sever,
>   Or the winding rivers be red;
>   They banish our anger forever,
>   When they laurel the graves of our dead!
>   Under the sod and the dew,
>   Waiting the judgment day;
>   Love and tears for the Blue;
>   Tears and love for the Gray.' "

Perhaps no one thing has done so much to soften the bitterness which civil war left in our country as the beautiful ceremonies connected with Memorial Day. As the years have gone on, and every Memorial Day the Southern soldiers have been more and more wont to cover the graves of their dead foemen with wreaths of Southern flowers, and again and again gray-haired veterans from both the " Blue and the Gray " have met beside the Hudson to do honor to the great commander who at Appomattox said, " Let us have peace," the coldness of suspicion and distrust have blown away, until, now that the boys from the South as well as from the North have marched together again under the old flag to fight a foreign foe, we see eye to eye.

The birth of Decoration Day deserves to be held in everlasting remembrance. Mrs. John A. Logan, the wife of the great Volunteer General, in company with some friends, made a trip to Richmond in March, 1868. Mrs. Logan was particularly impressed by the evidences of desolation and destruction which she witnessed everywhere, but which seemed to her to be particularly emphasized by the innumerable graves which filled the cemeteries, many of which were those of Confederate soldiers. In the summer before they had all been decorated by wreaths of flowers and little flags, all of which were faded, but which seemed to the tender-hearted woman to be a mute evidence of the devotion and

244

gratitude of those people to the men who had lost their lives to their cause.

On speaking of this to General Logan, on her return, he said it was a beautiful custom and one worthy to be copied, and, as he was then Commander-in-chief of the Grand Army of the Republic, that he intended issuing an order, asking the entire people of the nation to inaugurate the custom of annually decorating the graves of the patriotic dead as a memorial of their sacrifice and devotion to country. He issued the first order for May 30, 1868, and it was so enthusiastically received that Congress made it a national holiday.

It will thus be seen, that Memorial Day was born out of a partnership between a woman's tender heart and a man's noble purpose. It is also sweet to reflect that South and North united at its birth. The Southern mourners were the first to cover the graves of their dead with flowers, as they were the first to decorate the graves of their fallen foes; while their Northern brothers led in calling to it national attention, and made the custom as wide as the country. From henceforth we all unite in the closing couplet of Finch's noble song:—

> " Love and tears for the Blue;
>   Tears and love for the Gray."

JAMES THOMSON

RULE, BRITANNIA. c 1755

When Britain first, at heaven's command,
  Arose from out the azure main,
This was the charter, the charter of the land,
  And guardian angels sung the strain:
     Rule, Britannia,
     Britannia rule the waves,
     Britons never shall be slaves.

The nations, not so blest as thee,
  Must in their turn to tyrants fall,
While thou shalt flourish, great and free,
  The dread and envy of them all.
     Rule, Britannia,
     Britannia rule the waves,
     Britons never shall be slaves.

Still more majestic shalt thou rise,
  More dreadful from each foreign stroke;
As the loud blast that rends the skies
  Serves but to root thy native oak.
     Rule, Britannia,
     Britannia rule the waves,
     Britons never shall be slaves.

Thee, haughty tyrants ne'er shall tame;
  All their attempts to bend thee down
Will but arouse thy generous flame,—
  But work their woe and thy renown.

Rule, Britannia,
Britannia rule the waves,
Britons never shall be slaves.

To thee belongs the rural reign,
    Thy cities shall with commerce shine;
All thine shall be the subject main,
    And every shore encircles thine.
        Rule, Britannia,
        Britannia rule the waves,
        Britons never shall be slaves.

The Muses, still with freedom found,
    Shall to thy happy coasts repair,
Blessed Isle! With matchless beauty crowned,
    And manly hearts to guard the fair.
        Rule, Britannia,
        Britannia rule the waves,
        Britons never shall be slaves.

—*James Thomson.*

The poet Southey declares that this noble ode in
honor of Great Britain will be the political hymn of
that country as long as she maintains her political
power. It had a peculiar origin. Dr. Thomas
Arne, the great musical composer, composed the
music for his *Masque of Alfred*, and it was first
performed at Cliefden House, near Maidenhead, on
August 1, 1740. Cliefden was then the residence
of Frederick, Prince of Wales, and the occasion was

to commemorate the accession of George I. and in honor of the birthday of young Princess Augusta. Doctor Arne afterward altered it into an opera, and it was so performed at Drury Lane Theater on March 20, 1745, for the benefit of Mrs. Arne. In the advertisement of that performance Doctor Arne specially announces that *Rule Britannia*, which he calls " a celebrated ode," will be sung. We judge from this that it had even at that time gained great popularity.

Dr. Thomas Arne himself had a very interesting story. He was the son of a wealthy upholsterer in London and was born in 1704. He was educated at Eton, and his father intended him for the law, but while in school he had such a craving for music that he would often dress himself in servant's livery and sit in the upper gallery at the theaters. He learned to play with the strings of his spinet muffled in a handkerchief. One day his father attended a musicale at the house of a friend, and to his great astonishment and disgust, his own son occupied the place of first violinist. The father, however, decided to make the best of it, and not to fight against nature. From that time on the music-loving boy was allowed to play at home, and it was not very long before the whole family were proud of his achievements. He was the first English composer to rival Italian music in compass and difficulty. Doctor Arne lived and died absorbed in musical tones. Death came to him in the midst of his work, March 5, 1778. While attempting to illustrate a musical idea, he sang an air in faltering tones; the sound grew fainter, until song and breathing ceased together. Perhaps if he could have chosen his way to die this would have pleased him best of all.

The words for this *Masque of Alfred*, in which *Rule Britannia* appears, were written jointly by James Thomson, the author of *The Seasons*, and David Mallet, a Scotch tutor. It is not certain who was the author of these verses, Thomson, or Mallet. During Thomson's life in the newspapers of the day he alone was mentioned as the author. He died in 1751, and Mallet brought out, in 1755, his *Masque of Britannia*, at Drury Lane Theater, and it was received with great applause. The *Monthly Review*, a Scottish magazine of the time, in noticing it says: "*Britannia*, a Masque set to music by Doctor Arne. Mr. David Mallet is its reputed author. His design is to animate the sons of Britannia to vindicate their country's rights, and avenge her wrongs." On the whole, the weight of evidence seems to be in favor of the famous ode having been written by Thomson, but no one will ever be able to prove certainly as to whether it originated in his brain or Mallet's.

Rule Britannia soon became a favorite with the Jacobite party. Many parodies of it have been written, some of which were very famous in their time. One is to be found in *The True Royalist*, a

THE TOWER OF LONDON

collection of English songs long since out of print, which is perhaps worth repeating here: —

" Britannia, rouse at heav'n's command!
    And crown thy native Prince again;
Then Peace shall bless thy happy land,
    And Plenty pour in from the main:
Then shalt thou be — Britannia thou shalt be
From home and foreign tyrants free.

" Behold, great Charles! thy godlike son,
    With majesty and sweetness crown'd;
His worth th' admiring world doth own,
    And fame's loud trump proclaims the sound.
Thy captain him, Britannia, him declare!
Of kings and heroes he's the heir.

" The second hope young Hero claims,
    Th' extended empire of the main;
His breast with fire and courage flames,
    With Nature's bounds to fix thy reign.
He (Neptune-like), Britannia, will defy
All but the thunder of the sky.

" The happiest states must yield to thee,
    When free from dire corruption's thrall;
Of land and sea thou'lt Emp'ror be,
    And ride triumphant round the ball:
Britannia, unite! Britannia must prevail,
Her powerful hand must guide the scale. "

There is still another parody, also once very famous, contained in the book referred to. The first verse is as follows,—

" When our great Prince, with his choice band,
   Arriv'd from o'er the azure main,
Heav'n smil'd with pleasure, with pleasure on the
     land,
   And guardian angels sung this strain:
Go, brave hero; brave hero, boldly go,
And wrest thy scepter from thy foe."

In letting the parodies die, and in retaining the original song, succeeding generations have manifestly ensured the survival of the fittest. There has perhaps been no time since the Revolutionary War when Americans have listened to *Rule Britannia* with as sympathetic ears as since the beginning of our war with Spain. The almost universal sympathy expressed for us by all classes in England has served to bring the two nations closer together than a hundred years of ordinary intercourse. Whether or no it brings about the Anglo-American alliance so widely discussed, it has made *Rule Britannia* a grateful song to patriotic Americans.

OTTO EDUARD LEOPOLD VON BISMARCK·SCHÖNHAUSEN

THE WATCH ON THE RHINE.

Like gathering thunder spreads a cry,
Like clash of arms when battle's nigh,
The Rhine! there's danger to the Rhine!
Who'll shield it from the foe's design?
    Dear Fatherland, no fear be thine,
    Dear Fatherland, no fear be thine,
    Steadfast and true, we guard our German Rhine!
    Steadfast and true, we guard our German Rhine!

The tidings flash through million hearts,
From million flaming eyes it darts;
Our valiant sons, in danger strong,
Will guard our hallow'd stream from wrong!

What though the foe my life should quench,
I know thy wave will ne'er be French;
And ample as thy tide of blue,
The living stream of heroes true.

The shades of heroes past and gone
Upon our deeds are looking down;
By home and Fatherland we swear
The foeman from thy banks to scare.

While through my veins the life is poured,
As long as I can hold a sword,
No stranger shall our land despoil,
No foeman desecrate our soil.

Proclaim the vow from shore to shore,
Let banners wave and cannons roar,
The Rhine! The lovely German Rhine,
To keep it Germans all combine.

> Dear Fatherland, all fear resign,
> Dear Fatherland, all fear resign,
> Stout hearts and true will keep watch on the
> Rhine,
> Stout hearts and true will keep watch on the
> Rhine.

> *—Max Schneckenburger.*
> *(Translated by Lady Natalie MacFarren.)*

The Watch on the Rhine was written by Max Schneckenburger in 1840, and though not so fine a poem from a literary standpoint as many others that have embodied the same sentiment, it has about it that nameless charm which has enthralled the popular heart. Although it was thirty years old in 1870, it then struck its first great popularity and became by all odds the most popular war song in Germany.

Schneckenburger, like many another hymn writer, owes his entire reputation to a single song. He was an obscure Swabian merchant, quiet and unassuming, who never did anything in his life to attract public attention except to write this hymn. But it might well be said that in order to make a man's name immortal he need not do anything else than write one song that voices the soul's ambition or the heart's longing of a great people. Max Schneckenburger is perhaps the only writer of a popular national hymn who is not the author of other lesser songs; for we have not been able to discover that he ever published anything except *The Watch on the Rhine*. He died in Berne, in 1849, without the slightest thought that his song would ever make his name famous. Long after his death a handsome monument was built above his grave at Thalheim, in Wurtemberg.

The music for *The Watch on the Rhine* was composed by Carl Wilhelm, who first arranged it as a chorus for male voices. Wilhelm was a music teacher and conductor. He was born at Schmalkalden and died in 1873. Carl Hauser says that Carl Wilhelm never dreamed of *The Watch on the Rhine* turning out to be a national hymn at the time he composed the music. Wilhelm was a thorough Bohemian, a sort of typical German bandmaster, who was accustomed to write music on lagerbeer tables amid the fumes of smoking pipes. He was not counted as a great musician, except among a few bosom friends, and was satisfied to get a very small price for his compositions, and what he received in that way usually went to pay his beer bills.

On a certain occasion a schoolmaster who was a friend of Wilhelm asked him as a personal favor to compose a chorus for his pupils to sing on Commencement Day. The school-teacher saw the value of the music, and treacherously sold it. Thousands of copies went all over the world, but Wilhelm received no benefit therefrom. But after his music became famous, in 1870, tardy recognition was granted him, and in 1871 he was granted an annual pension of seven hundred and fifty dollars. He only lived two years to enjoy it.

In the Franco-Prussian war of 1870, *The Watch on the Rhine* had for a time a rival in a song the first verse of which ran: —

> " It never shall be France's,
>   The free, the German Rhine,
> Until its broad expanse is
>   Its last defender's shrine."

But when Von Moltke and old King William, with Bismarck and the Crown Prince Frederick, pushed their armies over the Rhine toward Paris, the warlike *Watch on the Rhine* soon distanced all other songs in the affections of the soldiers, and became the song of the nation.

Perhaps this martial song was never sung under more splendid circumstances than at the unveiling of the great National Monument inaugurated in 1883 to commemorate the victories in the Franco-Prussian war and the foundation of the new German Empire in 1870-'71. This magnificent monument stands on the bank of the Rhine opposite the beau-

tiful town of Bingen, famous in history and story, on a wooded hill nearly a thousand feet above the sea level, and flanked with glorious vineyards. No national monument is a more perfect expression of the spirit of a great people. The principal figure is a noble female form, thirty-three feet in height, Germania, wearing an imperial crown, and holding a sword wreathed with laurel as an emblem of the unity and strength of the empire. The figure is the embodiment of self-conscious dignity and strength. As a recent American traveler philosophizes, there is nothing vain or conceited about it, but the pride and confidence of one that knows and feels his power. The form erect and standing boldly forth as if before the face of the whole world, the head gracefully poised — thrown a little back, not haughtily nor disdainfully, but with steadfast and self-reliant courage — seems to say, "Behold in me the symbol of a great and mighty people!" On the right hand of the central figure, but far beneath its feet, is a symbolical figure of War, winged, with a helmet on its head, and a trumpet at its mouth, expressive of Titanic energy, as if a single blast of the trumpet would bring a million men in arms to the front. On the left is a symbolical figure of Peace, smiling benignantly, and holding in her arms the emblems of industry. These figures seem to say to the world, and especially to France, "War, terrible and destructive, if we must; but Peace, if you will."

265

In the hearts of the thousands of Germans gathered to unveil this great monument, there must have been a thrill of electric energy as they sang the popular song which it incarnated, for it stands as the crystallized representative of *The Watch on the Rhine.*

LA FAYETTE

THE MARSEILLAISE.

Ye sons of France, awake to glory,
Hark, hark what myriads bid you rise,
Your children, wives, and grandsires hoary,
Behold their tears and hear their cries!
Shall hateful tyrants, mischief breeding,
With hireling hosts, a ruffian band,
Affright and desolate the land,
While peace and liberty lie bleeding?

  To arms! To arms, ye brave!
  Th' avenging sword unsheath!
  March on, march on, all hearts resolved
  To victory or death.

Now, now the dangerous storm is scowling
Which treacherous kings, confederate, raise;
The dogs of war, let loose, are howling,
And lo! our fields and cities blaze.
And shall we basely view the ruin,
While lawless force, with guilty stride,
Spreads desolation far and wide,
With crimes and blood his hands embruing?

With luxury and pride surrounded,
The vile, insatiate despots dare,
Their thirst of power and gold unbounded,
To mete and vend the light and air;

Like beasts of burden would they load us,
Like gods would bid their slaves adore:
But man is man, and who is more?
Then, shall they longer lash and goad us?

O Liberty! can man resign thee!
Once having felt thy gen'rous flame?
Can dungeon, bolts, and bars confine thee,
Or whips thy noble spirit tame?
Too long the world has wept, bewailing
That falsehood's dagger tyrants wield;
But freedom is our sword and shield,
And all their arts are unavailing.

—Claude Joseph Rouget de Lisle.

This is perhaps the most famous song in the world. Not because it is sung more frequently than any other song, but because it has about it in title, romantic story, and fervor, something that has touched the heart of mankind and inspired for it a respect and admiration in all civilized lands.

Its author, Rouget de Lisle, was a young artillery officer who had a fancy for newspaper writing, and had contributed a number of articles to a newspaper in Strasburg owned by the mayor of the city. He dined one evening at his great friend's house, and the conversation turned on the departure of several hundred volunteers from the town of Strasburg to the Army of the Rhine. There were to be public ceremonies connected with the departure of the troops, and Mayor Dietrich urged young De Lisle to write a martial song to be sung on that occasion. He consented and went at once from supper to his room. The weather was bitter cold, but he sat down at the piano, and between reciting and playing and singing, eventually composed the *Marseillaise*, and, thoroughly exhausted, fell asleep with his head on his desk.

In the morning he handed the song complete, with words and music, to his friend, Baron Dietrich. Every one was enchanted with the song, and was roused by it to the greatest enthusiasm. It was sung a few days later at the departure of the troops from Strasburg, and thence to the insurgents of Marseilles, and soon to all the nation. In six months it had been adopted by the people, the army, the legislature, and the whole country. Its appeal to liberty and glory voiced the hunger of the popular heart at the time, and never did song so completely charm and capture an entire people.

De Lisle's mother was a most ardent royalist, and when the hymn was on everybody's lips, asked of her son, " What do people mean by associating our name with the revolutionary hymn which those brigands sing?" De Lisle himself, proscribed as a royalist, when flying for his life in the Jura Mountains, heard it as a menace of death, and recognizing the air as that of his own song, asked his guide what it was called. It must have seemed to him that day like a Nemesis of his own creation. It had then been christened *The Marseillaise Hymn*.

De Lisle was reduced to great poverty in later years. It is characteristic of the French nation that, a short time before his death, when poverty and age had crushed out the hopes and ambitions of life and he was no longer capable of receiving great joy from any honor that might come to him, the National Government decorated him with the ribbon of the Legion of Honor. It will no doubt do the same thing for Émile Zola. Not long after this tardy recognition, several pensions were conferred upon him, which he lived to enjoy but for a few months. He died in 1836.

The English translation of the *Marseillaise* as here given was published in 1795, only three years after the original was written. The translator's name is unknown, but it is considered the best English version.

The popularity of the song has naturally led to a great many claimants concerning it, especially the music. The author of a book entitled *An Englishman in Paris*, relates a very interesting story of a certain Alexandre Boucher, an eccentric violinist, who vowed that he (Boucher) wrote the *Marseillaise* for the colonel of a regiment who was about to leave Marseilles the next day. According to this story, Boucher was seated next Rouget de Lisle at a dinner party in Paris some years after the *Marseil-*

VIEUX PORT, MARSEILLES

laise had become famous throughout the world. They had never met before, and the violinist was very much interested in the gentleman whom, with many others at the table, he complimented on his production; only Boucher confined himself to complimenting him on his poem. "You don't say a word about the music," Rouget replied, "and yet, being a celebrated musician, that ought to interest you. Do you not like it?" "Very much indeed," said Boucher, in a somewhat significant tone. "Well," continued de Lisle, "let me be frank with you; the music is not mine. It was that of a march which came heaven knows whence, and which they kept on playing at Marseilles during the Terror when I was a prisoner at the fortress of St. Jean. I made a few alterations necessitated by the words, and there it is." "Thereupon," says Boucher, "to his great surprise, I hummed the march as I had originally written it. 'Wonderful!' he exclaimed; 'How did you come by it?' When I told him," says the violinist, "he threw himself round my neck, but the next moment he said: 'I am very sorry, my dear Boucher, but I am afraid that you will be despoiled forever, do what you will; for your music and my words go so well together that they seem to have sprung simultaneously from the same brain, and the world, even if I proclaimed my indebtedness to you, would never believe it.'" "Keep the loan," was Boucher's magnanimous reply. "Without your genius, my march would be forgotten by now. You have given it a patent of nobility. It is yours forever.''

All this is very interesting, but, unfortunately for Boucher's claim, De Lisle had put the music and the words together before the Reign of Terror began, and the story must fall to the ground.

Under the monarchical governments in France the song has always been held seditious, because of its extraordinary influence upon the French people. The first time since the Revolution that it was not regarded as treasonable by those in authority was at the opening of the World's Fair in 1878.

CHARLES EDWARD STUART, THE PRETENDER

THE BLUE BELLS OF SCOTLAND.

Oh! where, tell me where, is your Highland laddie
    gone?
Oh! where, tell me where is your Highland laddie
    gone?
" He's gone with streaming banners where noble
    deeds are done,
And my sad heart will tremble till he come safely
    home,
He's gone with streaming banners where noble
    deeds are done,
And my sad heart will tremble till he come safely
    home.''

Oh! where, tell me where, did your Highland lad-
    die stay?
Oh! where, tell me where, did your Highland lad-
    die stay?
" He dwelt among the holly trees, beside the rapid
    Spey,
And many a blessing followed him the day he went
    away,
He dwelt beneath the holly trees, beside the river
    Spey,
And many a blessing followed him the day he went
    away.''

Oh! what, tell me what, does your Highland laddie
    wear?
Oh! what, tell me what, does your Highland laddie
    wear?
" A bonnet with a lofty plume, the gallant badge of
    war,
And a plaid across the manly breast, that yet shall
    wear a star,
A bonnet with a lofty plume, the gallant badge of
    war,
And a plaid across the manly breast, that yet shall
    wear a star."

Suppose, ah, suppose, that some cruel, cruel wound
Should pierce your Highland laddie, and all your
    hopes confound;
" The pipe would play a cheering march, the ban-
    ners round him fly,
And for his king and country dear, with pleasure
    would he die,
The pipe would play a cheering march, the ban-
    ners round him fly,
And for his king and country dear, with pleasure
    would he die.

" But I will hope to see him yet in Scotland's bonnie
    bounds,
But I will hope to see him yet in Scotland's bonnie
    bounds;

His native land of liberty shall nurse his glorious
  wounds,
While wide through all our Highland hills his war-
  like name resounds,
His native land of liberty shall nurse his glorious
  wounds,
While wide through all our Highland hills his war-
  like name resounds.''

Annie McVicar Grant.

The father of Annie McVicar was an officer in
the British army and was transferred to this coun-
try for service in the American Colonies in 1757.
When he left the old country with his troops his
little daughter was but two years old. Soon after
he went away the little girl wandered from home
one day, greatly to the alarm of her family. She
was overtaken by a friend, and when asked where
she was going said, '' I am going to America to see
papa.''

In 1758, the mother and little girl crossed the
ocean and landed at Charleston, finding still a long,
tiresome trip to make before they rejoined the be-
loved soldier father, who was stationed at Albany,
New York. Here it was, in this then frontier land,
that Annie grew to girlhood. She had only two
treasures besides Indian trinkets and relics of Scot-
land, and these were Milton and a dictionary. She
committed *Paradise Lost* to memory, and the blind

poet's good and evil angels became as real to her as the soldiers about the fort. One day, when in the presence of Madame Schuyler, who was the great lady of Albany at that time, the little girl made a very appropriate quotation from Milton which so delighted the fashionable woman that thereafter she showed the child much kindness and regarded her as though she had been her own daughter.

When Annie was thirteen years old her father was transferred again to Scotland, and a few years later, at Fort Augustus, Annie McVicar fell in love with James Grant, the chaplain of the fort. She did her duty as a minister's wife, and one can imagine that she had plenty to do, as eight children came to their fireside, one after another, in rapid succession. Mr. Grant died poor, leaving his wife with these eight children dependent upon her. She must do something to make a living and keep the wolf from the door, and in her sore straits she gathered up the poems which she had written from time to time, and successfully published them by subscription. Afterward she brought out several volumes entitled *Letters from the Mountains*, which passed through several editions and brought her considerable profit. These fairly launched her on the sea of authorship, and many volumes of prose and verse followed, which, together with a pension granted her by the government, placed her in most comfortable circumstances, and she reached the ripe age

STIRLING CASTLE

of eighty-four, surrounded by a large circle of admiring friends in the city of Edinburgh.

Mrs. Grant wrote *The Blue Bells of Scotland* on the occasion of the departure of the Marquis of Huntly for the Continent with his regiment of Highland troops in 1799. A book entitled *The North Country Chorister*, printed in 1802, included this song under the title *The New Highland Lad*. Ritson, the editor of this book, says: "The song has been lately introduced upon the stage. It was originally *The Bells of Scotland*, but was revised by Mrs. Jordan, who altered the words and sang them to a tune of her own which superseded the old air." When Charles Mackay and Sir Henry Rowley Bishop were arranging old English airs, this song came under discussion. Mackay says: "*The Blue Bells of Scotland* is almost invariably spoken of as a Scottish air; but Sir Henry found reason to suspect that it was English, and urged me to write new words to it, to dispossess, if possible, the old song of Mrs. Jordan. He was induced to form this opinion by receiving from Mr. Fitzgerald 'a Sussex tune' to a song commencing: 'Oh, I have been forester this many a long day.' Three or four bars of the melody were almost identical with the second part of *The Blue Bells of Scotland*, but as the remainder bore no resemblance to that popular favorite, and the whole tune was so beautiful that it was well worth preserving, I so far complied with Sir

285

Henry's wish as to write *The Magic Harp* to Mr.
Fitzgerald's kind contribution to our work. Sir
Henry wrote under date of the 22nd of October, 1852,
'I am strongly of the opinion that when Mrs. Jor-
dan composed the music of *The Blue Bells of Scot-
land*, she founded the air upon that rescued from
oblivion for us by Mr. Fitzgerald — or rather that
she originally intended to sing it to that tune, but
finding some parts of it too high for her voice, which
was of a very limited compass, she altered them, and
the air became that of *The Blue Bells of Scotland*.' "

Mrs. Grant's *Highland Laddie* and Mrs. Jordan's
Blue Bells of Scotland have kept time together so
long now, that it is not likely any musical critic will
ever disturb them again. The following altered
version of Mrs. Grant's song has in some places
been even more popular than the original : —

" Oh where, and oh where is your Highland laddie
  gone?
' He's gone to fight the French for King George
  upon the throne;
And it's oh! in my heart, how I wish him safe at
  home.'

" Oh where, and oh where does your Highland lad-
  die dwell?
' He dwells in merrie Scotland, at the sign of the
  Blue Bell;
And it's oh, in my heart, that I love my laddie well.'

"What clothes, in what clothes is your Highland
    laddie clad?
'His bonnet's of the Saxon green, his waistcoat's
    of the plaid;
And it's oh! in my heart, that I love my Highland
    lad.'

"Suppose, oh, suppose that your Highland lad
    should die?
'The bagpipes shall play over him, I'll lay me
    down and cry;
And it's oh! in my heart, that I wish he may not
    die!'"

RUDYARD KIPLING

RECESSIONAL.

God of our fathers, known of old —
  Lord of our far-flung battle line —
Beneath whose awful Hand we hold
  Dominion over palm and pine —
Lord God of Hosts, be with us yet,
Lest we forget — lest we forget!

The tumult and the shouting dies —
  The captains and the kings depart;
Still stands thine ancient sacrifice,
  A humble and a contrite heart.
Lord God of Hosts, be with us yet,
Lest we forget — lest we forget!

Far-called our navies melt away —
  On dune and headland sinks the fire —
Lo, all our pomp of yesterday
  Is one with Nineveh and Tyre!
Judge of the nations, spare us yet,
Lest we forget — lest we forget!

If, drunk with sight of power, we loose
  Wild tongues that have not thee in awe;
Such boasting as the Gentiles use,
  Or lesser breeds without the Law —
Lord God of Hosts, be with us yet,
Lest we forget — lest we forget!

For heathen heart that puts her trust
  In reeking tube and iron shard—
All valiant dust that builds on dust,
  And, guarding, calls not thee to guard—
For frantic boast and foolish word,
Thy mercy on thy people, Lord!
                   Amen.

                 —Rudyard Kipling.

Queen Victoria's Diamond Jubilee, celebrated on the 22nd of June, 1897, has gone into history as the greatest human pageant in the whole story of humanity. As sovereign of Great Britain and Ireland and Empress of India, she occupies the most powerful position on earth. In addition to the material power represented, the admiration and love in which she is held by the truest people of every nation and kindred, because of her wise reign as well as her long and pure life, swelled her jubilee into a tribute of the united affection of civilized mankind. Preparations were made for months beforehand. Representatives from kings and presidents, as well as from the army and navy of every country in the world, came to do her homage.

It was not only Queen Victoria's day, it was Great Britain's day. Not only in London, where the great procession of representatives and soldiers from all the Colonies marched in honor of the gracious queen, but the services in honor of the day belted the globe. They began in the Colonies of New Zealand and Australia; afterward in South Africa; and so they followed the sun westward. When his light had crossed the ocean and reached the continent of America, the citizens of St. John's, Newfoundland, recommenced the anthem which was taken up in succession, in town after town across the continent through Canada, from the Atlantic to the Pacific. The loyal dwellers at Victoria, British Columbia, tossed it across the Pacific, and on to India, throughout all the Colonies of the empire of the Union Jack.

It was a sublime and unparalleled occasion, and yet it is not too much to say that the most splendid and perhaps the most enduring souvenir of the Queen's Jubilee was Rudyard Kipling's poem — the *Recessional*. The editor of the London *Times*, in which journal it was first published, declares that it is the greatest poem of the century, and it is quite possible that such may be the verdict of the next generation.

This great poem came at the close of the Jubilee exercises and struck the world with a surprise. While Mr. Kipling has long been regarded as a great writer of fiction, and a strong poet, the deep note of strength, the undertone of volcanic earnestness, as well as the profound religious faith of the *Recessional*, were qualities which had not been attributed to Mr. Kipling by the majority of people. Yet, as

Dr. George Horr, one of our brightest editors, has clearly set forth, Kipling, both as novelist and poet, has always portrayed the manly, strenuous side of life. He does not falter at putting before us ugly representations of vice, but beneath all the roughness and viciousness of men whom he describes, he reveals to us the real bedrock of genuine manliness. He never seeks to make us admire a cheat, a sneak, or a mountebank of any kind. Even in his most unconventional stories there is a Puritan strain in his temper, both in mental and moral quality, which holds him to the great essential moralities.

It is certainly appropriate that such a man should have eyes to see the profound religious side of the Queen's Jubilee, for at the bottom, everything that is real, that is manly and heroic, is also religious. It is not to be marveled at that this keen student of human nature and of human history should have been able to perceive that "the far-flung battle line," "the dominion over palm and pine," "the tumult and the shouting," "the captains and the kings," and "the far-called navies" are only dust and ashes, unless God lives in the hearts and controls the character of those who wield these instruments; and that "the frantic boast," and "the foolish word" may pull a national structure down upon the heads of a people drunken with their own power and riches. The sublime and solemn refrain of the poem,—

HOUSES OF PARLIAMENT

" Lest we forget — lest we forget,''

called back not only the British people in all parts
of the world, but the conscience of all civilization,
to the one abiding source of human power.

The fact that Kipling's poem touched the heart
of the English-speaking world as nothing else con-
nected with the Jubilee did, is, as Doctor Horr states,
" a profound testimony to the existence and domi-
nance of the religious instinct in the Anglo-Saxon
race. We have often been told that luxury, and
pride, and gross materialism, have quenched the
Puritan spirit. We have never believed that,
though it has been hard sometimes to maintain the
contrary against almost overwhelming evidence.
But under the breath of a moral issue the smoulder-
ing fire has leaped into flame. The poet who elicits
this temper, interprets it to itself, and gives it form
and voice, renders a service to the higher interests
of the race that can hardly be computed. Religion
has not lost its hold when such lines as these are
universally recognized as the noblest feature of the
Jubilee :—

" If, drunk with sight of power, we loose
   Wild tongues that have not thee in awe;
Such boasting as the Gentiles use,
   Or lesser breeds without the Law —
Lord God of Hosts, be with us yet,
Lest we forget — lest we forget!

297

" For heathen heart that puts her trust
  In reeking tube and iron shard —
All valiant dust that builds on dust,
  And, guarding, calls not thee to guard —
For frantic boast and foolish word,
Thy mercy on thy people, Lord. ''

Mr. Edward Bok, the brilliant editor of the *Ladies'
Home Journal*, secured the service of the celebrated
composer Reginald de Koven to compose suitable
music for this poem, and it was published in that mag-
azine in the issue for May, 1898.   De Koven's music
promises to be a great success.   On last Memorial
Sunday, May 29, the *Recessional* was sung to De
Koven's music by church choirs in every large town
and city in the United States.   Surely nothing could
be more appropriate for Americans to sing at the
present time than the *Recessional*.   It is a time
when it is important that the citizens of our proud
Republic shall remember that not in her vast terri-
tory, or inexhaustible wealth, or in mighty navy or
splendid army, but in the blessing of Almighty God
lies the real strength of a nation.   Kipling's august
prayer and refrain is as appropriate for us as for
Great Britain: —

" Lord God of Hosts, be with us yet,
  Lest we forget — lest we forget! ''

Lightning Source UK Ltd.
Milton Keynes UK
UKHW050344081218
333216UK00031B/2770/P